ᴬᵀHOME
ᵂᴵᵀᴴ
JESUS

AT HOME WITH JESUS

Contemplation and Scripture

TOM O'HARA SJ

Aurora Books
David Lovell Publishing

First published in 1998 by
Aurora Books
300 Victoria Street
Richmond Victoria 3121

in association with
David Lovell Publishing
PO Box 822
Ringwood Victoria 3134

Cover illustration: Jan Vermeer (1632–1675), *Christ in the House of Mary
and Martha*, c. 1655. Oil on canvas, 160 x 142 cm. National Gallery of
Scotland, Edinburgh.

Design by David Lovell
Typeset in 11/14 Adobe Garamond
Printed & bound in Australia

National Library of Australia
Cataloguing-in-Publication data

O'Hara, Tom, 1932–.
At home with Jesus: contemplation and scripture.

ISBN 1 86355 061 5.

1. Catholic Church – Prayer-books and devotions – English.
I. Title.

242.802

Nihil obstat: Peter Beer sj
Imprimatur: + Most Rev. David Walker

Acknowledgements
The material in this book was first published as part of the series 'When
you pray' by Tom O'Hara sj in *Messenger* and *Madonna* magazines

Foreword

THE 'MANY MANSIONS' OF JESUS' Father's house assure us of the spaciousness of God's saving love. All are to be included; there is always room for even the least of his friends for whom he is preparing a place so that they may dwell with him where he is, in the bosom of the Father.

In the more transient dwelling of this life too we might say there are many rooms, not so much with regard its spaciousness as to its complexity and diversity. Physical, emotional, intellectual and spiritual spheres all have their myriad roles in the life of each person. But how to put it all together?

The challenge is to open the doors of one sphere of experience to another, to let the light from each shine into the others, so that there are no disconnected, lost and darkened rooms. We need to recognize the doors and passages so that it is not all just a random maze with the occasional blocked corridor.

It is this disconnectedness which makes for so much of the modern human experience of fragmentation and isolation, such that existence itself may seem to be, in St Augustine's dark phrase, a *regio dissimilitudinis*, a place of unlikeness, alien and unfitting.

Our spiritual life is not immune from such complexity. There are manifold ways in which religious meaning comes to us. But none is so crucial as the immediacy of God's grace, that unexpected stirring of the holy Presence within, sometimes scarcely recognized, but capable of awakening us to the contemplative search and encounter.

Does this Presence have a form? Can we name it? The Scriptures, and preeminently the proclamation of Christ, mediate and identify that living Presence for us, as does the unfolding of the church's doctrine and the testimony of the faith-experience of the saints. Or, rather, they can and should fit together like this, not just 'logically', but with a living resonance and mutual illumination.

We can find ourselves 'at home' in any of these rooms—familiar texts, moral convictions, ways of prayer. The reason for that, as Tom O'Hara shows, is the living presence of Jesus who, wondrously, proves to be not just a companion in the house but himself our *regio similitudinis*, our very dwelling place.

Ross Collings OCD

Contents

Introduction

IT IS A COMMONPLACE TO SPEAK OF the thirst of people on the verge of the third millennium for a genuine encounter with God. There are so many obvious signs of the dying of religion as we have known it in the twentieth century. This is no cause for alarm for anyone in touch with the central mystery of Christianity: that it is only through death that new life can come about. We seem to be witnessing the death of a religion of highly developed structures founded on a very satisfying intellectualization of the mysteries of Faith. This has led many of the great people of our time to call for a religion of a more personal involvement, a return to our contemplative roots to re-discover the God revealed in Jesus Christ as available to anyone who will turn to God in sincerity of heart.

The late twentieth century has been the time of the discovery of the deeply personal. It has been an age of increasing freedom and opportunity, so that existing structures and practices are no longer sufficient to respond to need of persons to be intimately involved with their God.

In the field of theology, Karl Rahner and Bernard Lonergan have proposed that authentic theology is not a science alongside other human sciences but must be founded in personal conversion and a contemplative experience of God at work in the life of the theologian.

Mother Teresa of Calcutta called the world back to the meeting of Christ in the poorest of the poor. The liberation theologians are not interested so much in speculative theology as in the transforming power of the Good News. In the field of spirituality Tony de Mello has gone beyond the practice of 'spiritual exercises' to the encounter with God in the richness of the human psyche, the stories of all traditions and an authentic experience of the divine.

Since *Divino afflante spiritu* (1943) scripture scholarship has been both profound and comprehensive. Yet, sadly, the vast riches that have been opened up have not 'filtered down' to those wonderful persons, the long-suffering church-goers in the pews. Sometimes the scholars themselves have lost their way among the linguistics and form criticisms, so that the spirituality of the Word has not been broken open for God's People.

It is the scope of this small book to take some of the insights of scripture scholarship and apply them to the prayer life of the 'ordinary' man and woman of today. There are many thousands of contemplative persons we pass by in the street every day. Contemplation is not something rare or exceptional. We are all called by the fact of our creation to be contemplative.

Our thirst for contemplative experience of our God can be satisfied in many ways, as God freely chooses to gift each of us. It is a fact that the way of God's choosing is through personal involvement with Jesus, the Son of God, revealed to us through the Gospel. The Word of God leads us into the deepest depths and up to the greatest heights of contemplation. Here we will explore, as simply as possible, some of the treasures present for us in that Word. We shall then turn to look at a few of the greatest contemplatives in our Christian tradition, to see how their teaching is nothing other than a fulfilment of what is available to all of us in the contemplation of the Jesus of the Gospel.

The Gift of
Contemplation

A GENERATION OR TWO AGO THE
spontaneous reaction of people on hearing the word 'contemplation'
was to think of the great contemplative religious orders, like the
Cistercians or Carmelites. Contemplation was regarded as something
special and esoteric, to which the 'ordinary' Christian could not as-
pire. With the renewal of spirituality over the past forty years, we have
become increasingly aware not only that contemplative prayer is possible for all praying persons, but that contemplation is a natural gift
given to everyone on the planet.

Long before it is applied to prayer, contemplation is a very important attitude and activity of every human person. The word means
that aspect of our knowing that involves taking a really long look
at something or somebody. A baby becomes fascinated by a rattle,
a toy, its own toes. It looks and looks, touches, hangs on to the
loved item. It seems never to tire of returning again and again to
explore those toes. Here we see contemplation already at work. It
gives us a kind of knowledge that may not involve having a lot of
information about the object. Rather we have an immediate
contact at depth with the reality we contemplate. We become absorbed in it.

Contemplation is a most important activity for little children. To contemplate is to delight in. Watch a three-year-old frolicking with a puppy, trying to catch seagulls, suddenly stopping, its attention caught and absorbed by something, and you are seeing contemplation in action.

The word contemplation derives from the Latin words for 'with' and 'temple', a sacred area of earth long before it came to mean a sacred building. Contemplation is a remaining with the sacred, and we need often to remind ourselves that all of reality is sacred. To 'be with' is to be present, open, aware, focused, in touch, in communion with.

We all know many moments of being deeply touched by something or somebody. But how hard it is for us to linger, to prolong those moments. I look forward to meeting an old friend I haven't seen for years. There is a moment of delight when we meet, but often we find ourselves after a short time bored, wanting to be distracted, to look away.

The ability to contemplate is a gift. When it is given, I become absorbed in the other, more and more fascinated. Time doesn't hang heavily. I feel as if I could stay forever. This often happens in conversation with somebody I love, with a friend, or even with somebody I don't yet know well. There is more than a 'meeting of minds'. We seem to be really one. Intimacy makes us one in mystery. The way into intimacy is the way of contemplation.

The situations that we find contemplative are limitless and very diverse. A conversation, sitting in silence with somebody, a shared smile with a passing stranger, a visit to someone in hospital, a walk in the bush, gazing at a sunset, walking beside the sea, struggling to solve a problem, working, becoming involved in a hobby, embroidering, painting, singing, making a hole-in-one. The list is endless.

What do all of these have in common? There is a sense of immediate and deep contact with reality . I am caught out of myself. 'Whoever loses their life for my sake will find it.' This is the beginning of the experience of ecstasy.

The gift of contemplation differs from a material gift, in that it is not given once and for all to be possessed. It is essentially an inner gift, to be responded to, exercised and developed. The exercise of this gift requires that I be truly present to the reality contemplated. This demands that I be disciplined, reflective, capable of inner silence, stillness and solitude. These qualities imply a 'gathering together' of a person's inner resources, so that there is freedom to be engaged with the object of contemplation.

The word 'contemplate' developed from its original meaning (see above) and came to mean to consider, to ponder, to gaze at. Gazing can be a very demanding activity. To gaze I must be present and interiorly still enough to remain present. It involves a looking that is spread out in time, much more than a fleeting glance. And what we say about looking applies also to touching, hearing, smelling and tasting.

The use of the senses, along with imagination, art, music, story and poetry, give us a natural entry into contemplation. All of these activities have an immediacy of contact with the matter contemplated. Intellectual knowing is usually abstract, 'at one remove'. We think *of* something, rather than become immediately involved with it. Not that the intellect is alway barred from contemplation. Because of the unity of the human person, the understanding can lead us into heart knowledge, in which we seem to 'grasp' some truth with both immediacy and depth.

For a contemplative experience to occur, there is a moment of initial contact, an attraction drawing me out of myself. Sometimes, without any effort on my part, this moment will prolong itself and I will be carried along very easily into contemplation. At other times I will need to make an effort to 'stay with' the object of contemplation. A frequently reported experience is that after some time, say fifteen minutes, people tend to become bored. If they then force themselves to stay, the boredom suddenly disappears, the sense of delight returns and it is very easy to stay for a long, long time.

It is commonplace to speak of the hectic pace of modern life as being the enemy of presence. The demands to be somewhere else seem to be instant and endless. To be so hectic is to lose the ability to stop, to think, to enjoy intimacy. Paradoxically it is this hectic activity that is leading people to recognize their thirst for contemplation. In the climate of compulsive modern living, the need for contemplation is being more and more acutely felt.

As well as the felt need and the initial attraction drawing us into contemplation, we can experience initial reluctance. A vague intuitive awareness of the necessity of letting go of our own ego can stop us entering into contemplation, even though we may have experienced great joy previously in contemplating the same subject. And this battle between attraction and reluctance can continue during a contemplative experience. We simultaneously want to stay with the profoundly delightful experience, and to run away, to abandon the contemplation which seems so demanding.

In order to contemplate, we must 'be with'. Our stance before reality becomes one of presence, awareness, relationship, communion, entry into mystery, heart knowledge, intimacy, enlightenment, wisdom.

Presence is much more than simply being in the same geographical location as the other. Presence implies the gathering together of my inner self so as to direct my consciousness towards the other, and then to hold it there. As this happens, and the reality contemplated becomes the focus of my attention, my awareness is heightened, so that I am in touch with the being of the other.

When we are truly aware of reality, of an event, of a moment, we taste or savour that reality; we know it in depth. When unaware, we move rapidly and superficially from one object to another, with an absence of relish for any one of them. As we grow in awareness of the other, we become united through the gift of communion. Whatever the particular reality with which I commune, I become aware of being opened up to communion with Reality itself. I have entered into mystery.

Contemplation and mystery are correlative terms. Mystery is beyond the grasp of abstract, intellectual knowledge; it requires a special kind of knowing, and that knowing is called contemplation. The mystery of being is not known through rational analysis or intellectual discourse; it is known through heart knowledge, that kind of experiential knowing that cannot be conceptualized, and therefore cannot be verbalized. The experience of contemplation is much more likely to evoke a sigh or an exclamation of surprise and wonder than to lead to a lengthy discourse. The knowing involved is depth-knowledge, which is the meaning of the word 'intimacy'.

Contemplation is not a knowing of many things, but a way of knowing. An unenlightened knowledge may truly grasp its object; then a new light is made available, and enlightenment knows the same object in a new and enriching way.

Through the gift of wisdom we are enabled to bring together intellectual knowledge and the fruit of contemplation. We grasp the meaning of a particular truth, but we are simultaneously aware of its connection to greater Truth, so that the actual knowing of the particular truth becomes at the same time an entry into and a savouring of universal Truth.

'Wisdom stories' provide us with examples of the exercise of the natural gift of contemplation.. They tease our intellect by proposing a meaning that we can understand, but at the same time cannot fully comprehend. There is a second level of meaning not to be grasped, but to be contemplated. Because the understanding cannot comprehend the full meaning, awareness is automatically shifted to the heart. The young fish has heard about a wonderful place called the ocean, so asks the old fish where to find it. 'This is it; you're in it', is the answer. The young fish replies with disdain: 'This! This is only water; I'm looking for the ocean'. Continuing the same metaphor, non-contemplative knowing can be compared to looking upon the surface of the ocean from outside: contemplative knowing involves being immersed in it.

In contemplation there is a silence, a silence of the heart. This may involve in some measure the absence of thoughts, words, images, desires and actions. But the essence of this silence is not the absence of all words nor the cessation of all action, but an inner quality of awareness and consciousness that is present with or without thoughts, words, images, desires and activity. Certainly there will be an absence of analysis of what is contemplated, of making plans or speeches about it, of using it. The contemplative attitude is the opposite of that of the plumber who, on seeing Niagara Falls, said: 'I think I can fix that leak'.

In contemplation the other is received, but not possessed. I must allow the other to be in sovereign independence of my ego. Contemplation requires that I approach reality with profound respect, with submission, weakness and poverty of spirit. It can happen only to the degree that there is abandonment of self.

As the pace of modern living increases, and the opportunity for choice and mobility grows more and more rapidly, the human person experiences a radical alienation and yearns for quiet, stillness and contemplation. In this climate the search for a satisfying religion takes over. There is no need for us to turn to new or eastern religions to meet this need. Within our Christian tradition contemplation can enable us to develop attitudes in touch with all of the beauty of God's creation and with God.

Intimacy

FROM TIME TO TIME WE ALL HAVE THE experience of what it is like really to 'click' with another person. The time, the place, the atmosphere, how we are feeling, all seem to be just right. We fall into conversation. There is a sense of ease and relaxation. Neither of us wants to to be anywhere else, to rush or to interrupt. We become very comfortable with pauses and silences. The experience is quiet, gentle, profound and joyful.

The sort of experience just described is usually unexpected, unpredictable. I can't make it happen. It is clearly a gift. It may occur with a life-long companion or a comparative stranger. Intimacy which is attained with a long-term friend or partner has a distinctive quality different from that of intimacy with a new friend or 'stranger'. In our humanness we require time to grow in relationship. The depth of relating can be built up, slowly and at leisure. The deeper our knowledge of the other person grows, the further we realize there remains to go. We are vaguely aware of the infinite dimension of the other which can never be exhaused by our knowing. While this is true, there is also the 'Romeo and Juliet' experience, love at first sight, which immediately possesses a quality of completeness and commitment that will never be revoked.

Intimacy may be one-to-one or in a group. In the group situation each one of us seems to be keenly aware of each of the others. A surprising sensitivity develops. The usual sense of competitiveness, wanting to 'get in and have my say', disappears. There is a profound respect. Each one feels a real sense of freedom, knowing that the others are all ready to listen attentively whenever one chooses to speak. There is a meeting, even a 'wedding', of minds. All self-preoccupation vanishes as I enter the life of the other. I seem to be lifted out of myself—which is literally what is meant by the word ecstasy.

Words we use to describe this kind of experience are empathy and intimacy. The first means entering into the experience of another, as distinct from sympathy which means experiencing *with* the other. Intimacy literally means depth. Through intimacy the human spirit is drawn into the spirit of another. The physical obstacle of our material nature seems to be overcome as spirits become deeply united. The human person is a mystery, unable to be known, grasped or comprehended as a scientific, historical or mathematical reality can be. Intimacy or communion is a special kind of knowledge that gives us immediate contact with the depths of another person.

If intimacy is a gift, is there anything we can do to make it happen? Certainly. We can be aware of and avoid the obstacles to intimacy. Unfortunately the pace of our modern lives is particulary geared to providing these obstacles. It becomes very difficult to experience intimacy when we are too busy, too hectic, too objective, scientific, technological and task-oriented.

To be people capable of intimacy we need to be able to leave aside work and really to play. By play is not meant devoting time to a sport or game in which the rules are all strictly defined and the main task is to win. To play is to be child-like, to allow the rules of the game constantly to change, to be challenged to continual adaptation to the other players and the shifting circumstances of the game, to leave myself behind, to be caught up into the adventure of providing a joyful experience for all the participants.

When we have re-found our childhood capacity for play, we need to take one more step before we are ready for true intimacy. We need to be willing to leave play aside, and simply to be with the other person, to 'do nothing' together. We waste time in one another's presence. We are now ready to receive the gift of intimacy, should it be given.

We have all experienced intimacy, both in given moments and in life-long relationships. Yet the nature of the case is such that we need continually to re-learn the lesson about what is involved. Our capacity for relationship and for intimacy is unlimited. There is an infinity about it. It is not a question here of quantity, but of quality and of depth.

It seems hardly necessary to draw the parallel between our human relationships and our prayer life. The human experience of intimacy corresponds to what in prayer terms is usually called con-templation. We experience it in a fleeting moment, or in a prolonged time of prayer, or in a life-time of commitment and relationship with the Lord. We are constantly called to be our true selves, to 'become as little children', to be simple, trustful, open and playful in his pres-ence. Then we are ready to 'waste time' with him and enter into deeper and deeper communion.

It is usually necessary to prepare for the reception of this gift of intimacy through praying often: by making the effort involved in pay-ing attention to the Lord in faith. This enables us to 'let go' of the disturbing demands made by our ego or self-centredness. We learn to attend more and more to the presence of our loving God. God be-comes the focus of our interest. We are ready to give ourselves to the effort of thinking about the ultimate truths of our human existence. We have entered upon a path which, in Christian tradition, is usually given the name 'meditation'.

At this stage prayer is not just a matter of reciting vocal prayers, but a constant readiness to turn towards God, who has now become the centre of much of our thinking. These steps—letting go of self, praying frequently, and thinking more and more about God—are the ones usually required to prepare us for that intimacy which has been traditionally called contemplation or contemplative prayer.

Contemplative Prayer

IN THE PRE-VATICAN II CHURCH IT WAS
not uncommon for people to be told to say their prayers with the help
of *The Key of Heaven* or their rosary beads, and to leave contemplation
to those called to the contemplative religious orders. In recent years
there has been a remarkable change. With the general popularity in
our time of spirituality and meditation, many people are setting aside
a time of half an hour or more for daily prayer, and are finding that
within a few months they are moving towards a new kind of contemplative prayer. This is fully in keeping with the Carmelite tradition.
John of the Cross expects that a novice who perseveres in prayer for a
period approaching a year will pass through the preliminary stages of
meditation into contemplation.

What, then, do we mean by contemplation? In the Christian
tradition the word has had many varied meanings. Primarily it is a
natural gift which enables us to be truly present to reality, to commune with the real world in a way that is beyond mere rational thought
or feeling. People readily understand that to remain in silence before a
vivid sunset is a contemplative experience. Any deep presence to God's
creation is a true act of contemplation. Our attention can be caught
by something ordinary—a tree, a mountain, a river—or something

tiny—a flower, an ant, a leaf—and we become present and focused, and, for a short time at least, contemplative.

The longer we stay with the object of contemplation, the deeper our attitude goes. I may not remember clearly the details of what I have seen or heard, touched, tasted or smelt. It is not rational knowledge, or sense or imaginative knowledge that is important here, but rather an experience. I may retain only a vague sense of presence, but I know that I have been in communion with reality.

What we have said about contemplating nature applies, of course, to our contemplation of events and persons, even that strangely mysterious person, myself. Obviously a mother in giving birth has a new experience of reality that is too deep for words. A death in the family, a great celebration, a major item of world news, or something tiny like an intimate smile is each a natural occasion of contemplation.

That ever-changing, vague, intuitive awareness of myself which is the condition of all my other relationships with reality is itself a reality that cannot be put into words. More than that, it cannot be grasped by the understanding. What the psalmist refers to as 'the wonder of my being' is a mystery than invites me to be contemplative. It should be fairly obvious how the elements of this 'natural' contemplation carry over into our prayer life. The same key words—reality, presence, experience, mystery, communion—are applicable.

Just as the 'natural' contemplation puts us in touch with the deep and mysterious being of the object contemplated, so contemplative prayer is the way of being in touch with spiritual realities, which even more than natural realities are deep and mysterious and inaccessible to the senses, feelings, imagination and intellect. It is not that these faculties have to be suspended in order to contemplate. They may or may not be more or less active. The essential element is that there is something happening on a deeper level, something that cannot be explained, only hinted at.

A striking example of the parallel between natural contemplation and contemplative prayer is provided by the experiences of the Buddha (Siddhartha Gautama, of the sixth century BC) and St Ignatius Loyola, of the sixteenth century. Exhausted by many spiritual exercises performed over several years of quest for enlightenment, the

Buddha sat down under a bodi tree and was gifted with *enlighten-ment*; he suddenly saw all of reality in a new light, at a new depth, with a new sense of communion.

Ignatius relates in his autobiography that after a few months of spiritual exercises following his conversion 'he sat down for a little while by the river which was running deep. While he was seated there, the eyes of his understanding began to be opened; though he did not see any vision, he understood and knew many things, both spiritual things and matters of faith and learning, and this was so great an *enlightenment* that everything seemed new to him. Though there were many, he cannot set forth the details that he understood then, except that he experienced a great clarity in his understanding. This was such that in the whole course of his life, through sixty-two years, even if he gathered up all the many helps he had had from God and all the many things he knew and added them together, he does not think they would amount to as much as he received at that time'.

The mystical experience was for Ignatius the gift of enlightenment, as it had been for the Buddha. Where the two differed is that the content of Ignatius's experience was expressed in terms of Christian revelation.

The practice of contemplative and mystical prayer, and reflection upon the experience, has had a long and rich history from the earliest years of Christianity to our own day. Through the centuries a vast array of different, and often overlapping, terminologies have been used to describe the progressive conversion and transformation of the praying person into ever deepening union with God. While the modern tendency is to move away from analytical terminology, like 'acquired' and 'infused' contemplation, the reality remains of a gradual decrease in the activity of the praying person and a growing openness to God's activity in one's prayer and life.

It may be helpful to bear in mind that there are two great traditions of contemplation which are not contradictory but complementary. The first, the *kataphatic* tradition, approaches contemplation in terms of affirmations that can be positively made about God. The earliest representative of this tradition is Origen (died 255) who is often referred to as the theologian of light. For him there are three steps in the return of fallen humankind to the contemplation of God. The first is moral illumination, the second natural contemplation, the third the contemplation of Godself. The movement is towards greater and greater light. This tradition is represented in Julian of Norwich, Ignatius of Loyola and Teresa of Avila.

The second tradition, the *apophatic*, approaches contemplation from the standpoint that God is infinitely beyond all human knowing, so that our communion with God in love must advance through the denial of the possibility of knowing. The early representative of this tradition, Gregory of Nyssa (died 395) also presents three steps, but for Gregory these lead into deeper and deeper darkness. He draws upon the example of Moses who first met God in the light of the burning bush (Exodus ch.3), but then in the darkness of the cloud (Exodus ch. 19), and finally in deep darkness (Exodus ch. 33). The apophatic tradition is represented by the 'Mystical Theology' of Pseudo-Dionysius (5th century), *The Cloud of Unknowing* and John of the Cross.

A modern focus for understanding what is meant by contemplation has been provided for us in the *Catechism of the Catholic Church* (1994) in its article entitled 'Contemplative Prayer' (paragraphs 2709–2724). Wisely the authors of this article do not attempt to provide an intellectual definition of contemplation, which, by its nature, escapes definition. Instead they give a broad spectrum of explanations of what contemplative prayer is.

The article describes nine different aspects of prayer that it declares to be contemplative. In five of these, key words are ones used in our previous chapter on 'The Gift of Contemplation' (pp. 3–8). Contemplative prayer is a gift (2713); it is a gaze (2715); it is hearing (2716); it is silence (2717); it is a communion (2719). There is an old theological axiom that grace perfects nature. Grace and nature really do work together. Grace is operative in, with and through nature.

Perhaps surprisingly, the catechism starts its treatment of contemplative prayer with a quote from the Autobiography of St Teresa of Avila in which she describes it as 'nothing else than a close sharing between friends; it means taking time frequently to be alone with him who we know loves us'. The element of surprise may come in the catechism's choice of such a simple, warm, positive description of contemplation rather the more analytical, austere, negative definitions current in the pre-Vatican II era.

In paragraphs 2712, 2713, 2714 and 2717 the article draws attention to the Trinitarian character of contemplative prayer. The mystery of the Trinity, so often regarded by simple people as far removed from them, something to be talked about only by professional theologians, turns out to be most practical in the life of every Christian.

Rightly so. There is nothing remote about our sharing through Baptism the life of Father, Son and Holy Spirit. Each time we pray we activate the potential of this life within us. Our communion with the Trinity becomes more truly effective in forming us in God's image.

In praying contemplatively we are simply building on the scriptural and theological foundations of contemplation. The instruction of Jesus to his disciples in Matthew 28:19 is to baptise people into the life of Father, Son and Holy Spirit. The Spirit given to us in Baptism makes us brothers or sisters of Jesus and adoptive children of the Father. This is the teaching of Romans chapter 8 and Galatians chapter 4. The Holy Spirit, united to our human spirit, cries out within us 'Abba! Father!'.

The same Holy Spirit prays within us in a way that can never be put into words. When we pray, we are activating the gifts of the Holy Spirit, a theological reality based upon the text of Isaiah 11:1-3. The gifts are translated in the revised ceremony for confirmation as 'wisdom, understanding, right judgment, courage, knowledge, reverence, wonder and awe in God's presence'. Through the gift of the Spirit we are born anew (Jesus to Nicodemus in John ch. 3).

Our Baptism springs from the mystery of the death-resurrection of Christ. In Baptism we enter the tomb with him, so as to rise to new life (Romans 6:3-11). Through the indwelling of the Spirit of the risen Lord we are not only adopted as sons and daughters of the Father, but we become one with Christ. John presents this theme throughout chapters 14 to 17 of the gospel, and in the first letter. Jesus abides in us and we in him. Jesus and the Father come to us to make their home in us. The same theme of living within is used by Paul to express our union with the risen Lord: 'I live, now not I, but Christ lives in me' (Galatians 2:20). Paul exclaims mystically: 'For me to live is Christ' (Philippians 1:21).

To engage in contemplative prayer I must come not only as a child of God, but as a forgiven sinner (2712). The key, foundational grace of Christian life is that of conversion: the acknowledgment of one's sin and of the impossibility of saving oneself; the personal acceptance of the redeeming love of Christ crucified. The reception of this grace sets a person free from self-serving attitudes, free to become a disciple in response to the now ever-present love and call of Christ. The way of discipleship is the way of contemplation. Having consciously appropriated the Christ-life in Baptism, a person puts on the mind and heart of Christ through contemplative prayer. This is summed up in the centrepiece of the catechism's article: 'Contemplation is a gaze of faith fixed on Jesus' (2715). These words provide a summary of our next chapter: 'Contemplation and the Gospel'.

A contemplative heart is a listening heart. Hence the importance of 2716: 'Contemplative prayer is hearing the Word of God'. Once again the description is surprising in its simplicity and availability to all. The hearing involved is, of course, not just with the ears but with the heart; it requires our attentive listening and our response; it is capable of growing indefinitely in depth.

'Contemplative prayer is silence' (2717). The silence referred to is an inner silence, the silence of the heart. The article makes it beautifully clear that words and contemplation can be present simultaneously. 'Words in this kind of prayer are not speeches; they are like kindling that feeds the fire of love.' It is sometimes said that contemplation is a way of praying without words, thoughts or feelings. Far better to call it that dimension of our praying which is deeper than words, thoughts or feelings.

It is not the absence or presence of words that is the key, but their quality. St Teresa of Avila recognized this. She writes in *The Way of Perfection* about a sister who could not master any techniques of meditating, so was reduced to continually reciting the Lord's Prayer, and in this way reached the highest levels of contemplation. It is that prayer that takes us to the heart, the deepest part of ourselves, the centre of our being. So, good news for active and busy people: contemplation does not necessarily require withdrawal from all other activities. A person who has developed this gift becomes habitually contemplative, so that there is a 'space' inside them that can be frequently touched, no matter how pressing or stressful their situation may be.

Confronted with the hectic pace of modern living, more and more people are finding the need to be reflective and in touch with the world of spirit. The more they do this, the more they find that they are drawn to read books like *The Cloud of Unknowing*, or the writings of contemplatives like Julian of Norwich, John of the Cross or Thomas Merton. These works turn out to be not too deep and incomprehensible, but in tune with the experience of modern people of prayer.

The goal of contemplative prayer is union with God in Christ. For all contemplatives the way to this union is the way of love. As the catechism puts it in its summary of the article on prayer: 'Contemplative prayer is a silent love' (2724). The union is objectively given in God's commitment to each of us in creation and Baptism. It is personally, subjectively appropriated through the experience of contemplation. Experience is not the goal, but a means to that deeper liberation that makes our union with God effective in our living. As Teresa writes at the end and climax of her journey into the 'Interior Castle', this effectiveness will show itself in love for our neighbour through service.

Contemplation
and
the Gospel

SINCE VATICAN II, PRAYING WITH THE
Scripture, previously a rarity among Catholics, has become commonplace. The result is a real renewal and deepening of contemplative life
for many people. When we take up the Scripture to pray, the obvious
place to start is with the gospels. As I do this, two complementary
elements are at play: first, opening my heart to the Word which speaks
to me personally in the power of the Spirit, communicating to me the
Christ-life it contains; second, my growing knowledge and appreciation of what the gospels are and how I can use them most profitably.
Clearly the first element is the more important, but the second has its
significance.

An obstacle to our praying with the gospels is the misunder-
standing that the four evangelists were interested in writing a biography of Jesus, a history of his life and times in the sense in which we
understand history today. For them the chronology and geography of
his life were very secondary, and could be treated with great freedom
in accordance with their essential purpose which is theological and
spiritual. Each of the gospel writers in his own way sets out to tell us

who Jesus is: not so much who Jesus was when he walked our earth, but who he is personally for the writer and his community. The gospels are essentially stories about the risen Christ, who was operative in the life of the Christian community of the time at which they were written, meeting their needs. The same risen Christ is at work in each of our communities today, meeting our needs.

Once we have grasped this basic understanding of a gospel, we are liberated from the old 'harmony' mentality, the attempt to make one continuous, coherent 'life of Christ' out of what are four different works, each inspired by the Holy Spirit, and each to be respected in its own unique individuality. Instead of throwing the four gospels into a 'melting-pot', we now have four presentations of who Jesus is, each of them enriching our personal relationship with him.

The Spirit who inspired the gospels was well aware that no one written word could capture the infinite variety of the face of Christ, so we have been given four different portraits. In so far as we are in touch with each of them in its distinct individuality, our whole relationship with the Lord grows richer. It is somewhat like our way of using different artistic representations of Jesus. We can contemplate the Lord, as the artist intended, with the help of a Byzantine icon. We relate differently in contemplating a Renaissance work, like the crucifixion by Guido Reni. We may have a third experience of the Lord in contemplating a modern work like that of Georges Rouault. We have no photograph of Jesus; the diversity of portraits enriches our contemplation of him in ways that a photograph could not.

An awareness of whether it is the Jesus of Mark, Matthew, Luke or John can be a great help, as we will see later, but the first essential is that I be present to him as the passage I have in hand reveals him to me. There are many ways that the passage I have chosen can touch me. It may lead me to reflect on my life, offer me healing or forgiveness, console me, call me, challenge me; the possibilities are endless. But the basic power of the Word is to put me in the presence of the risen Lord who is drawing me into closer relationship with the Father through the Spirit.

In its first document, that on the sacred liturgy, the Second Vatican Council expanded the previously accepted understanding of the words 'real presence'. 'Christ is always present in his church, especially in her liturgical celebrations. He is present in the Sacrifice of the Mass not only in the person of his minister, 'the same now offering through the ministry of priests, who formerly offered himself on the cross', but especially in the eucharistic species. By his power he is present in the sacraments, so that when anybody baptises it is really Christ himself who baptises. He is present in his word, since it is he himself who speaks when the holy scriptures are read in the church. Lastly, he is present when the church prays and sings, for he has promised 'where two or three are gathered together in my name, there am I in the midst of them' (Matthew 18:20). It is precisely the presence of the risen Lord in his word that enables us to be present to him, really to encounter him when we take up the gospels in prayer.

Prayer is a personal meeting with God. This meeting takes place in and through Christ. We meet Christ in the Gospel. The gospels are the Good News of the risen Lord Jesus active in our lives today. We meet him today. We grow in faith, in hope, in love, in trust, in friendship whenever we read and ponder the words of the Gospel. The daily reading of the gospels puts the reader in touch with the Lord Jesus. This is why praying the Gospel is such an important way of praying for a Christian.

The greatest gift we have from God is the gift of our Baptism, leading, of course, to its climax in the Eucharist. Through Baptism we receive the gift of the Spirit of the risen Lord Jesus. That Holy Spirit makes us one with him. The same Holy Spirit cries out in our hearts: 'Abba! Father!' (Romans 8:15, Galatians 4:6). This leads St Paul to the paramount truth of our adoption as sons and daughters of the Father.

Here we have the theological roots of all Christian contemplation. For all the great mystics, contemplation is that gift of prayer that wells up from within. If we are authentically present to the Jesus of the gospels, we are not just exercising our imagination, but are contemplative in the strictest sense of the word. Nothing in Christian contemplation or mysticism can ever go beyond the contemplative doctrine of St Paul and St John. To be contemplative is to be *at home with Jesus,* as in John chapters 14 to 17:

'If anyone loves me and keeps my word, my Father will love

them, and we will come to them and make our home in them' (14:23).

'Make your home in me, as I make mine in you' (15:4).

'If you remain in me and my words remain in you, you may ask what you will and you shall get it' (15:7).

'Father, may they be one in us, as you are in me and I am in you. With me in them and you in me, may they be completely one' (17:21-23).

Or, in the first letter of John: 'Those who live in love live in God and God lives in them' (1 John 4:16).

Paul has the same contemplative theme of life: 'I live, now not I, but Christ lives in me.' (Galatians 2:20). 'For me to live is Christ' (Philippians 1:21).

What we do in contemplation is appropriate in prayer and implements in our living the grace already present in the Gospel. The gifts expressed above by John and Paul are given to all the baptised through the indwelling of the Holy Spirit. That Spirit is the Spirit of the risen Lord, the Jesus with whom we are put into living, personal contact whenever we take up the gospels. Through our contemplation we appropriate the grace of our Baptism, so that it becomes more effective in its influence on the whole of our living: our thoughts and feelings, both conscious and unconscious, all our actions, even our bodies. We are gradually being transformed in fact into the 'other Christs' we already were truly, but potentially. Now that potential is being realized.

In this sense we are all called to be mystics. This is not some revolutionary, modern teaching. As long ago as 1926, Dom Cuthbert Butler concluded his classic work *Western Mysticism* by writing, 'We learn that mysticism, like religion itself, is within the reach of all: "It is not too hard for you, nor is it far off. It is not in heaven, that you should ask, who will go up to heaven to bring it down for us? It is very near to you, in your mouth, and in your heart, that you may do it"'. In the final quotation Butler is applying to mysticism the words of Deuteronomy 30:11-14.

In a more recent work (*Mystical Theology*, 1995), William Johnston refers to the universal call to mysticism expressed by Bernard Lonergan: 'The original and almost shocking thing in Lonergan is that he looks on mystical love as the goal and climax of human living. This love is the peak-point of the thrust towards self-transcendence and authenticity that is rooted in the minds and hearts of all human beings. There is nothing elitist about it. It is not a gift offered to Christians alone. It is not offered to religious people alone. It is offered to all men and women who would be fully human. Can we not conclude that for Lonergan there is a universal call to mysticism?'.

William Johnston himself had espoused the same postion several years earlier in his book *Being in Love* (1988) where he wrote, 'Mystical contemplation is not extraordinary, it is very ordinary. All Christians, I believe, are called to it; and when they follow this path, they become their true selves, their very ordinary selves'.

If we start our contemplation with the gospel of John, we are immediately plunged into the heart of the mystery of the Trinity, the Word who is God dwelling with God from all eternity. The only Son whose whole reality moves into the bosom of the Father (John 1:18) shares with us God's life. Through his story of the 'beloved disciple', who reclined on the bosom of Jesus at the Last Supper, John indicates that every disciple is to move with Jesus into the bosom of the Father. The beloved disciple remains anonymous for John as the type of every Christian disciple. This has always been recognized in Christian tradition in its understanding of the giving of Mary to be the mother of us all when Jesus, on the cross, entrusted her to the beloved disciple (John 19:26-27).

If we commence with Matthew or Luke, we are first invited to a loving presence to the Person of God-with-us or Salvation-for-the-People, who is present in our world, not in word or thought or action, but in the form of an infant. If we turn to Mark, we are present to the mystery of the Good News of God's Son (Mark 1:1), revealed first in his baptism. As we follow the dynamic of any of the four gospels, we are progressively challenged to deeper and deeper levels of contemplation. We are called to be engaged with Jesus in his ministry of teaching and healing, leading us always on to the mystery of the Eucharist, symbolically presented in the form of the feeding of the five thousand.

Mark and Matthew link this great eucharistic symbol to the striking nature miracle of walking on water, as the preludes to the great question Jesus poses: 'Who do you say that I am?'. Luke, in a famous 'omission' of much of Mark's material, goes straight from the feeding to the great question (Luke 9:18). For John the great question, in the form: 'Will you too go away?' (6:67), is in an even more explicit eucharistic setting (John 6:1-58). Mark in 7:14-27 has Jesus ask the disciples no fewer than nine times if they have managed contemplatively to penetrate the mystery of those actions of his that reveal his identity. Clearly, the great question itself is not seeking an intellectual answer, but a contemplative answer coming from the heart of each of us.

Immediately after Peter's response to the question of Jesus, the challenge to a radical new depth is proposed. Can they take on board the sayings about discipleship and the cross? These sayings are in no way open to human reasoning. It is only through contemplation in union with Jesus that we can begin to enter into the mystery of losing our life in order to find it. Closely linked to the predictions of suffering is the great scene of preparation for the Passion, the Transfiguration, once again inviting our contemplation.

When we come to the Lord's Passion itself, once again we are taken to a completely new level of contemplative prayer; all we can do is stay with him in profound silence. This is the only way into the real faith of the Roman soldier, who proclaimed, when he saw how Jesus died, 'Indeed this man was God's Son' (Mark 15:39). Finally, in the Resurrection we are called on to meet a Lord who is truly hidden in every aspect of our material creation (see Colossians 3:1-11). It is only the truly contemplative who can penetrate the veil of this hiddenness.

The Word of God contains within itself power to touch our hearts. That power is at its best when we are present to the person and message of Jesus of the gospels. This sense of presence is often revealed through my imagination. The gospels are each written in a style that is simple, concrete and imaginative. They are full of carefully crafted stories and powerful dramas, which have a power to draw the reader into the action.

When we read them carefully, slowly and attentively, it is not difficult to feel involved in what is taking place. I may form a visual picture of Jesus and the other characters involved in the scene. I may feel him touch me or hear him speak. More importantly, I have a sense of presence and relationship. This may not be clearly definable, but all of my previous experience of the Lord comes to life in my unconscious. Theologically, my baptismal relationship with him is activated and becomes more operative.

Jesus is truly our brother. There is a deeper reality, taking us further into the mystery. He and I are one. Now, while this oneness is an objective fact, it needs to be developed, to grow, to come alive in me. This is where a life of personal contemplation comes in. Through my contemplation I am present to the Christ-life within. I am in touch with the Lord. He is the same Lord Jesus who walked the roads of Palestine. The gospels reveal to us the truth of Jesus's life on earth; but they are far more than this. They are the communication of the life of the risen Lord. As I pray the gospels, I don't merely learn about a Jesus who lived a long time ago. I grow to be more like the Jesus who is alive today: in all of creation, in all events, in all persons, in me!

The truth which the Scriptures give us is, in the words of Vatican II, 'that truth which God wanted put into the sacred writings for the sake of our salvation'. While the gospels give us an historical setting and historical outline of the life of Jesus, they have very little interest in history as we understand it today. The gospels contain far more story than history. While history speaks to our intellect, stories touch and fire our imagination. As we ponder the gospels, our hearts are formed and shaped by the personality and inner life, the heart of the Lord. This takes place via our imagination.

Imagination here is not understood simply as the power to form inner sense images apart from external stimuli. Imagination opens to us the world of symbol, of deep feeling, of presence to another, of personal relationship.

Unfortunately our education has tended to downplay imagination. We were taught to believe that what is most real is what is materially most solid. Dreams and visions were often dismissed as '*only imagination*'. The truth is the reverse. Imagination is far more real than steel and concrete. It is more real because it puts us in touch with what is truly and fully human. In our imagination we are inspired and challenged. We dream dreams that lead us to go beyond our limitations to live in reality the kind of life Jesus lived.

The value of imagination in the Christian life is made specially clear in the stories of the birth and infancy of Jesus in the gospels of Luke and Matthew. John introduces his gospel with the famous prologue in the philosophical-theological language of 'the Word'. Luke and Matthew communicate who Jesus is by telling us beautiful, pictorial, imaginative stories. Luke's primary message is that Jesus is 'salvation for all the peoples'; Matthew's message is that he is 'God-with-us'.

The evangelists don't simply write these truths, but they fill our minds with images of angels, shepherds, the Temple, journeys, dreams, kings, wise men, precious gifts. As we fill our imagination with these symbols, the gospel truth is communicated to us on the deep level of the heart.

How and in what sense can I be present in prayer today to the Jesus who lived 2000 years ago? Perhaps I am a great admirer of Pope John XXIII. I remember what he looked like, his smile, what he said, his tone of voice, in fact the whole quality of his personality. I still know him. Death does not destroy authentic personal relationship. The same can be true of great historical figures or saints from eras even long gone, about whom I have read. The same is true of Jesus. The Spirit operates in, with and through the human, and in, with and through this human way of relating.

In 1992 a veteran of the Coral Sea battle takes the opportunity on the fiftieth anniversary to revisit the scene of that battle, which was decisive in the defence of Australia from Japanese invasion. He goes already armed with a cluster of memories. But, as soon as he arrives at the scene, more memories and images flood in. In imagination he sees again the position of the ships, the faces of his comrades, the bombs dropping through the air, the exploding vessels. He hears the sound of it all. He touches again his dying friend whom he had held in his arms. He grasps again the hands which had reached out to pull him from the water. He smells the explosives, the dead bodies, and tastes again the sweat, blood and tears. Many feelings are aroused in him. He experiences great emotion. He weeps again. But he experiences being carried beyond imagination and emotion into deeper feelings, like loss, grief, gratitude and love. He knows that he has entered into his heart, and remains a long time in profound silence. This experience will remain with him always and influence him for the rest of his life.

Here we have a striking example of the exercise of the natural gift of contemplation. We may ask whether, as our friend exercised this gift, the Coral Sea battle took place again. The stock answer is that objectively it did not, though subjectively for him it did. Yet there is a real sense in which the historical event is not simply past. He has relived through entry into contemplation something that has retained its existence as it has passed into eternity.

When we come to contemplate a mystery of the life of Jesus in the Gospel, all of the kinds of thing that our man experienced in his Coral Sea contemplation may happen to us. Grace truly builds on nature. Our contemplation in prayer takes place in, with and through the natural gift of contemplation. Yet there is something more here.

In presenting the contemplation of the Incarnation St Ignatius suggests that we be present to the Word who has just become incarnate for us. The perfect tense points us to the enduring presence of a past event, as in the threefold acclamation at the Eucharist: Christ has died, Christ is risen, Christ will come again. Christ died, but his death has effectively just happened now. Notice that we do not say 'Christ is dead'. His death has occurred, but is not simply over and done with.

Can we go further? Yes, we can. All the events of history have an eternal quality about them. There is the obviously discernible effect of the past: I am a result of my history; the child is father to the man. But over and above this, there is an abiding, eternal dimension to every human event. In the case of the Lord Jesus this is infinitely heightened through his Resurrection. Every event of his earthly history becomes eternally present through the transforming power of the Resurrection. This is why the author of the Book of Revelation writes of the Lamb that was slain now standing in the presence of the throne (Revelation ch. 5). The events of the earthly life of Jesus have gone forward into glory through the power of the Resurrection.

As the author of Hebrews puts it: 'Jesus Christ is the same yesterday, today and forever' (Hebrews 13:8). The evangelists convey the same truth when they have Jesus display his wounded hands and feet (Luke 24:39) and even his side (John 20:27). This is why the evangelist John can legitimately present the passion and death of Jesus as an activity of the risen Lord. Jesus goes forth in power to his suffering and death, and from the cross he hands over the Spirit. John is able to bypass a three-day wait for the resurrection, and a fifty-day wait for the sending of the Spirit.

Does this mean that, over and above their enduring presence, the events of the life of Jesus are actually happening now? It is utterly correct to speak of Jesus suffering now in his suffering members. But this does not mean that Jesus himself is suffering: 'The death he died he died to sin, once for all, but the life he lives he lives to God' (Romans 6:10). Contemplation takes place from the perspective of eternity. When I contemplate, I am in touch with the risen Lord in his mysteries. They are called 'mysteries', from the Greek verb 'to hide', because they have a hidden or deeper meaning.

So, as I pray in union with this risen Lord, the historical events of the life of the Lord are taking place within the perspective of this prayer. Yes, from the point of view of the praying person, he is being scourged now. This is why my experience of compassion or grief is not just some voluntaristic exercise in which I step outside present reality to pretend that something essentially past is in fact happening before my eyes. There is far more involved than a fanciful reconstruction through imagination of an event that remains essentially past. For me, as I pray, it is happening. This is amply confirmed in practice. Without the benefit of this theoretical understanding, this is precisely the experience reported again and again by those contemplating the mysteries of Christ as they make the full Spiritual Exercises.

The only facts concerning the childhood of Jesus that Luke and Matthew have in common are: the names of his parents, the virginal conception, that he was born in Bethlehem and grew up in Nazareth. They are far more interested in firing our imagination than in satisfying our curiosity. As we ponder the gospels, the same principle applies to the geography as to the history. It is not necessarily a help to the fruit of our contemplation to have visited Israel. We picture the scene in whatever way we wish. Nor do we have to be another Michelangelo. The 'pictures' can be extremely vague. What matters is the sense of *presence*.

As we pray the gospels in our imagination, we are doing what St Paul urges the Philippians to do: 'Whatever is true, whatever is honorable, whatever is just, whatever is pure, whatever is lovely, whatever is gracious, if there is any excellence, if there is anything worthy of praise, fill your minds with these things' (Philippians 4:8).

Whenever we read the stories of any great historical or fictional character, we form in our imagination a relationship with that person. We may see them, more or less clearly; we may hear the sound of their voice; but the essential thing is that we truly relate with them. The mention of their name evokes a whole series of associations that we have built up in our imagination. The gospels, like any great drama or biography, have the power to touch us in this way. They have an additional, far greater, power because they are not just human words but God's Word. The central character, Jesus, is not just a great man. He is the Lord, alive and well today. He and I are one through Baptism. So I don't just read *about* him. He speaks in my heart and relates to me from within the deepest part of my person. The Jesus of the Gospel is the same Jesus who is alive 'in all things' (Colossians 3:11) now. He is the same Jesus who is already at the end of history drawing the whole of it and all of us together into himself and so into the Father (see 1 Corinthians 15:28).

With this background in mind, we take up the gospels as the special way of growing in that intimacy with Jesus which we call faith. We begin with a prayer to grow in this faith and intimacy. It is the prayer of the musical, *Godspell*: to see thee more clearly, to love thee more dearly, to follow thee more nearly, day by day. The history of this little prayer goes back through St Ignatius to the English saint, Richard of Chichester (13th century).

After making this prayer, I begin to open my inner self to the Gospel and to Jesus whom it reveals. The simplest, most obvious and most helpful way to start to do this is by using my five senses. The senses are the faculties through which we have an *immediate presence to reality*. Can I see Jesus? Some texts of the Gospel may be especially good for this kind of prayer. For instance, in the fourth chapter of Luke, Jesus stands up to read and 'all eyes were fixed on him' (v. 20). These words may help me to focus my imagination on seeing Jesus. I may allow myself to be 'amazed at the gracious words that come from his lips' (v. 22). Or I may find it easy to see him in the crib at Bethlehem, or being carried by his parents up to the Temple for the Presentation, or walking the Galilean countryside, or getting into a boat ... Whatever the particular gospel scene, it is important to pause for a while to try to be with Jesus in my imagination.

The intimate knowledge of Jesus for which we asked at the start of our prayer is a 'heart knowledge'. It begins with my sense of being in his presence as I contemplate the gospel. Through this presence relationship grows. I become more like Christ, not in a sort of external imitation of him, but in putting on his mind and heart. I don't have to be working out in my head what the gospel is saying to me. It is sufficient to rest in the Lord's presence. He is his message. If I am truly in touch with him, I am really hearing the gospel message.

During this kind of imaginative praying with the Gospel I touch the Lord, just as he touched the leper in Mark 1:41, or as the penitent woman touched his feet in Luke 7:38. At Bethlehem I ask Mary if I may nurse the baby! I can also use the senses of taste and smell in a contemplative way. 'Taste and see that the Lord is good' (Psalm 34:8). 'Your robes are all fragrant with myrrh and aloes and cassia' (Psalm 45:8). The life of the Lord enriches the whole of my personality, including each one of the five senses. This kind of prayer gives me a sense that I have been in the presence of the Lord, and my life is being gradually transformed by the Word, in both its meanings, the Gospel and the Word-made-flesh.

The Scriptures continually instruct us to *listen* to God's Word. See the great prayer of Israel in Deuteronomy 6:4, or the words of Isaiah 55:2-3, and the constant references in all four gospels to hearing Jesus and listening to his words. I commence by listening carefully and attentively as I read the words. But it is important to go deeper, to allow the Word to 'sink in', to go down to that level understood by the word contemplation, where it is not so much the meaning of the words that nourishes my mind, but a taste for the Word which nourishes my heart. By constantly repeating in prayer the words of the Gospel I can learn them *by heart*. Then perhaps they well up from my unconscious at times when the Lord wishes to enlighten my daily life with the light of the Gospel.

As we continue to be present to the Lord Jesus through exercising the senses of our imagination, we grow in the grace of heart-knowledge, of love and of intimacy that we asked for at the start of our prayer. The more we allow this to happen, the more we are prepared for a mystical experience of that presence, love and intimacy. It is only right to expect this to happen at least occasionally. In this kind of mystical experience the inner senses of the imagination are overtaken by the 'spiritual senses'.

Throughout the tradition of Christian mysticism these 'spiritual senses' have been regarded as the human faculties used by God to communicate directly with the person at prayer. Nowhere is the teaching expressed more richly than by the great Franciscan, St Bonaventure:

'The soul believes in, hopes in, and loves Jesus Christ who is the incarnate, uncreated, and inspired Word, "the Way, the Truth and the Life" (John 14:6). When by Faith one believes in Christ, the uncreated Word and Splendour of the Father, the believer receives the spiritual sense of hearing and seeing: hearing the words of Christ and seeing the splendour of his light. When one desires the inspired Word, one recovers a spiritual scent through such desires and affections. When one embraces the Incarnate Word in love, receiving thereby light and ecstatic love from Christ, the lover has recovered spiritual taste and touch. Thus, with the spiritual senses reinvigourated, one can see, hear, smell, taste and embrace the Spouse.'

Over and above the sense of presence, we have the fact that Jesus speaks and acts in a way that proclaims a set of values, the 'gospel values'. Praying with the gospels brings home to me the love, courage, compassion, openness of Jesus, his thirst for justice and solidarity with the poor. I am challenged by the conditions of discipleship: the grain of wheat must fall into the ground and die. I am drawn to know and accept that I must follow him all the way to my own Calvary and my own Resurrection.

As we pray with the gospels, we come more and more deeply into the presence of the Lord Jesus. We are not merely reading the Gospel as we would read another book, to 'learn something', to 'discover the message'. We are present to a Person. We are present on the level of heart to heart. We are present to the Lord with whom we are already one. While this truth is basic and must always be at work as we contemplate the Lord in the Gospel, true Christian contemplation will never transport us into some heavenly, 'spiritual' world, out of touch with the realities of our human life at the turn of the millennium. The words of author Marshall McLuhan, 'The medium is the message', are eminently true of the Lord. We 'hear' his message in being simply present to his person. At the same time it is necessary to reflect on the teachings of the gospels and apply them to our own lives.

The Lord of the Gospel speaks in very clear terms to each person who today is willing to undertake the adventure of being open to his call. Some Gospel truths are basic to the life of every one of us. We are all called to be empty of self, as the Lord was (see Philippians 2:5-11). The Christian must be like Jesus, 'the man for others'. For all of us he proclaims the greatest commandment: love of God with our whole heart and of our neighbour as ourselves. We must even love our enemies. The way of the Gospel is the way of Jesus, the way of poverty of spirit. To be poor in spirit is to accept the whole reality of our humanness, our gifts and our shortcomings, strengths and weaknesses, joys and sorrows. Gospel persons do not try to escape from any aspect of life, or to anaesthetize or distract themselves from difficulty, pain and struggle. They embrace and celebrate their humanness to the full.

Every Christian must follow the Lord in rejecting the temptations to wealth, power and self-aggrandizement, and follow instead the way of spiritual poverty, service and humility. The beatitudes give us the 'charter of the Kingdom' which we are all called to live. In so far as we respond to their challenge and live by them, we receive God's blessing and find true happiness at the heart of self-sacrifice. The only way for any of us to join this Kingdom is the way of the little child. Every Christian must take up the cross daily and follow Christ: '*Everyone* who tries to save their life will lose it; *everyone* who loses their life for my sake will find it'. This is the only saying of Jesus which appears in all four gospels. It is found twice in Matthew and twice in Luke, so six times in all. It must be the essence of the Gospel message!

As we pray daily with the Gospel, we 'put on the Lord Jesus Christ' (Romans 13:14; see also Galatians 3:27). This happens in the depth of our heart, more or less unconsciously, through contemplation. At the same time, we become consciously more aware of fundamental Christian values as suggested in the previous paragraph. There is a third level of conversion that must also be attended to. Not only must I strive to say 'Yes' to the universal demands of Gospel values, but I must reflect carefully upon my own life to see how the Lord's message needs to be applied to all of the varying details my life today.

One of the healthiest movements in modern prayer is that of being free to express in our prayer exactly how we feel. We are encouraged to be more like the psalmist, who complained to God, became impatient and angry with God, and never tired of pouring out to God the details of what was going on in his life. In this way our prayer becomes more *real*. Through our modern education, means of communication and the media, every one of us is in touch with a vast network of complex realities that make up our lives. We bring into our prayer all our concerns—personal, family, global, business, political, social—and open ourselves to what the Gospel has to say in each of these areas.

As I pray in this way, listening to the Lord's message in the Gospel addressed to me personally in the whole of my real life situation, he will invite me to make real, practical decisions about how to live the Gospel. Because of the complexity of our lives today, it can be very necessary to seek some guidance in sifting what is truly significant in each one's Christian living. Members of various Christian churches are re-discovering the need and importance of spiritual direction for people committed to a life of prayer. As this need is being addressed, there is the growing possibility for each of us to find someone to help us in applying the Gospel to our lives and making truly effective decisions about living as a Christian today. Through this process the realities of our lives are progressively more united with the reality of the life of the risen Lord.

As we continue our contemplation of the gospels, right through the suffering and death of the Lord to his resurrection, our practical decisions about embracing discipleship are confirmed. We receive the strength to carry them out through the power communicated to us. Through this power we grow in the ability to live our whole lives in Christ risen, joyfully and productively for the coming of his Kingdom.

Praying with
Mark's Gospel

any gospel passage with a desire to grow in faith, in heart-knowledge
and relationship with Jesus, to put on more of his mind and heart.
The same Spirit who inspired the gospel text is present in us as we
ponder that Word, teaching us, enlightening us and forming us in the
image of Christ The more we are aware of the particular concerns of
each gospel writer and of the portrait of Jesus he offers us, the more
ready we are to allow the Spirit to work in us.

It is appropriate that we approach the gospel of Mark with a
sense of enthusiasm, even excitement. Most scholars believe that Mark
is the earliest of the four gospels. It is the foundational one, followed
closely by Matthew and Luke, and, less closely, by John. Even the first
verse of Mark suggests the opening up of a whole new world: 'The
beginning of the Good News about Jesus Christ, God's Son'. It is the
beginning (the Greek word is *genesis*), like the book of Genesis revis-
ited; and immediately Mark gives us the word 'Gospel' (Good News)
by which all four will become known forever.

The first words spoken by Jesus in Mark's gospel state his fundamental message with unique clarity, directness and power: 'The time
has come, and the kingdom of God is close at hand. Repent, and

believe the Good News' (1:15). The title Mark gives to Jesus, 'God's Son' (1:1), will be repeated at the key points of the gospel: the Baptism, where God announces to Jesus, 'You are my beloved Son'; at the Transfiguration, where God prepares the three disciples for the fullness of faith to be revealed in resurrection-through-suffering by the words, 'This is my beloved Son'; and finally at the Crucifixion, where the Roman centurion, seeing how Jesus dies, arrives at the faith foreshadowed in Mark 1:1 with the words, 'Indeed this man was God's Son' (15:39). This is the faith that Mark's gospel is designed to bring from the heart of each of his readers.

Of the four gospels, Mark's is the one which gives the most vivid details, presenting Jesus most clearly and earthily in his humanness. This allows Mark to bring out most strikingly the contrast with the divine action of Jesus, as in the storm at sea, where Jesus changes dramatically from a weary man asleep in the back of the boat with his head on a cushion to the one whom the wind and sea obey (Mark 4:35-41). So, if it is intimate knowledge of Jesus that we are looking for, Mark is the place to start. Matthew (God-with-us), Luke (the Saviour of the Peoples) and John (the Word of God) commence with theological reflections about who Jesus is. Mark starts quite simply, factually and abruptly, with the preaching of John the Baptist and the arrival of Jesus coming to be baptised.

At the baptism of Jesus, Mark gives us the first verse from Isaiah 42 which will become the text most quoted in the gospels, and he changes it in a very significant way (perhaps by combining it with Psalm 2:7, 'You are my son; today I have become your father') from the third person to the second: 'You are my son the Beloved; my favour rests on *you*'. Mark not only affirms that Jesus must begin his mission firmly rooted in the Father's word of love spoken to him, but at the same time invites his readers to begin the pondering of the life of Jesus by hearing the same words addressed to them.

Mark abounds in direct, colourful details absent from the other three. Here are just a few of the numerous phrases that are unique to Mark. Jesus took Peter's mother-in-law by the hand (1:31). Jesus was moved with pity (1:41). The leper began to talk freely about it. (1:45). He was at home (2:1). He sat at table in his house (2:15). They removed the roof (2:4). They took him just as he was (4:36). In the stern of the boat with his head on a cushion (4:38). Is not this the carpenter?(6:3). Among his own family (6:4). He laid his hands on a few sick people and cured them (6:5). He marvelled at their unbelief (6:6). The blind beggar of Jericho is named as Bar-timaeus (10:46). He threw off his cloak (10:50). Following these few examples, it is most instructive to take any passage from Mark's gospel and compare it carefully with the corresponding texts in the other three. It leads us into direct relationship with the Jesus who is so clearly pictured.

As the gospel moves towards its central turning-point—'Who do you say that I am?' (8:29)—Mark presents, in 6:30-6:56, a key passage, repeated by each of the other gospels, even John. In these stories of the feeding of the five thousand and the walking on water Mark is at his best in picturing for us the intimate, tender relationship of Jesus with his disciples and their fully human interaction. If we wish to be drawn into this kind of relationship with the Lord, we can do no better than to take up the sixth chapter of Mark for very careful reading and for contemplation.

We find in Mark's gospel a clear, central turning-point in the eighth chapter, when Jesus asks his disciples to declare their faith with the great question: 'Who do you say that I am?'(8:29). Up to this point the mission of Jesus is presented as being primarily one of healing and teaching with authority in order to lead people to faith. By faith the gospel means not so much an intellectual adherence to truths as a personal relationship with our Lord Jesus Christ. It is the personal acceptance of Jesus that brings people healing and salvation.

A typical response to the ministry of Jesus by its beneficiaries is to acknowledge him to be the Christ (Messiah). Jesus often replies to this by telling people to keep quiet about who he is. This already suggests what will be a key point for us as we pray with Mark, namely that there can be a naturalistic, 'human', unenlightened reaction to Jesus. For the contemporaries of Jesus this way of thinking was typified by their expectation of an earthly, political Messiah. This is highlighted in chapter 10 in the approach of James and John to Jesus to seek the most privileged postions in the glory of Jesus (10:35-45). The key to the gospel is to go beyond this spontaneous reaction to a deeper wisdom which penetrates the mystery of God's revelation in Christ. He cannot have a messianic identity apart from suffering and death.

The climax of the early ministry of Jesus, leading to the great question, is the double miracle or sign of feeding of the five thousand, a clear reference to the Eucharist in the taking of bread, blessing, breaking it and giving it, and the walking on water. This structure is followed by Matthew, by Luke, with the omission of the walking on water, and even by John, who is normally so different from the others.

John emphasizes the eucharistic significance of the feeding of the five thousand with the great discourse of Jesus on faith and the Eucharist in 6:32-58. It is precisely the Eucharist that is the focus of the great question for John in the form: 'Will you too go away?' (6:67).

Mark (8:1-10) and Matthew (15:32-39) underscore the importance of the feeding miracle by repeating it in the form of feeding four thousand, just before the question of Jesus, 'Who do you say that I am?' For Mark there are three different answers to this question: the unenlightened response of people in general saying that Jesus is 'John the Baptist, Elijah or one of the prophets', the incipient faith of Peter: 'You are the Messiah' and the definitive answer of God at the Tranfiguration: 'This is my beloved Son'.

John (6:26-27) and Mark (8:14-21) both underline the disciples' failure to understand the great sign. In the course of these few verses of Mark, Jesus asks his disciples nine different questions, in an attempt to 'wake them up', to bring them to awareness that they must question their 'human' way of thinking and look for that deeper meaning which requires a spiritual enlightenment.

When, in the eighth chapter, Peter acknowledges Jesus to be the Christ, Jesus replies by advancing the argument one step further and beginning for the first time to speak about his coming suffering, death and resurrection. Peter does not begin to understand, so that Jesus has to point out to him that his way of thinking is 'not God's but man's'. Here we are involved in the central message of Jesus about the struggle between good and evil. Peter's way of thinking is a sign of the work of the evil spirit. 'Get behind me, Satan!'

From this turning-point on, the gospel of Mark is dominated by the coming suffering, death and resurrection of Jesus. Just as the Baptism set the course for his whole mission, now there is a similar manifestation of the Father's presence, the Transfiguration, to introduce this new theme. At the Baptism the Father strengthened Jesus with his words of love. At the Transfiguration this word is addressed to us, the disciples, to help us begin to come to terms with the mystery of suffering and death. This is my beloved Son, Suffering Servant, the fulfilment of all that was promised to Israel in the Old Testament.

Mark makes it clear that Peter's acknowledgment that Jesus is the Messiah is only a preliminary step on the way to true faith. The real confession of faith will be made by the pagan, the Roman centurion, who is brought to this faith by the *death* of Jesus. 'When the centurion saw the way that he died, he said: 'Truly this man was God's son' (15:39).

The heart of the mystery to be contemplated is presented in chapters 8, 9 and 10. In each of these Mark gives us predictions of the Passion, and the great sayings about discipleship, including the only gospel saying of Jesus to be repeated by all the other evangelists: 'Whoever tries to save their life will lose it; whoever loses their life for my sake will find it' (8:35). Each time Jesus speaks like this the disciples are having an argument about who will be the greatest.

This is Mark's way of bringing home to us the contrast and struggle between the spirit of Jesus and the spirit of the unredeemed person. This is a battle-line that passes through the heart of each of us. It is the ongoing struggle of Christian living. There is no 'solving' this mystery. We are invited to contemplate it more and more deeply by taking to heart the central message of Mark's gospel.

Praying with
Matthew's Gospel

THE GOSPEL OF MATTHEW, WRITTEN
for a church of both Jewish converts and Gentiles, representing the
new, restored Israel, has a very distinctive Jewish flavour. Matthew
gives an interpretation of Jewish Law in which Jesus is the authentic
interpreter, emphasising mercy and justice as the criteria as to whether
any particular law is to be followed. Humanity is burdened, not that
the Law itself is a burden, but much of its interpretation is. Jesus
lightens this burden (Matthew 11:30). Like Mark, Matthew emphasizes the role of Jesus as teacher or rabbi. While following the basic
structure of Mark's gospel and repeating many of his stories, Matthew
uses another source of the sayings of Jesus to expand his teaching role
with five great discourses.

The five discourses are 1) chapters five to seven: the so-called
sermon on the mount; 2) the lengthy instructions to the twelve in
chapter ten before they set out on their mission; 3) the collection of
parables in the thirteenth chapter; 4) the discourse about the church
in chapter eighteen; 5) the final discourse of chapters twenty-three to
twenty-five. The number, five, is no accident. It is chosen by Matthew
to parallel the great teaching of the Old Testament in the first five
books of the Bible, the Torah or Pentateuch. It would be a mistake to

regard these writings of Matthew as each spoken by Jesus as one continuous sermon or instruction. They are very dense, containing much moral teaching, exhortation and threat of punishment. Taken in its entirety each of them can be very heavy reading. These sayings of Jesus should rather be used for prayer a little at a time. Then we find in them some of the greatest treasures of our Christian spirituality.

Other distinctively Jewish aspects of Matthew's gospel are its emphasis on community (Matthew is the only gospel which uses the word 'church'), and its constant reference to the fulfilment of the Old Testament.

Matthew presents Jesus to us as bringing to fulfilment the work of Moses, the great leader of Israel. As God's covenant with the people is formed, Moses goes up a mountain to receive from God the Ten Commandments, the tenfold ethical expression of God's life-giving Word. So, Jesus too goes up a mountain, not this time to receive, but himself to announce the Beatitudes. They proclaim the fundamental blessings of Christianity. Unlike the commandments, they do not come in the form 'Thou shalt not …', but 'Happy are those who …' Jesus is not so much a law-giver as the One who proclaims the authentic desires of every human heart.

In the fulfilment of these desires, we enter 'the kingdom of heaven', we are put into union with God. We experience true happiness. The Beatitudes are full of paradox. Those who mourn are proclaimed as happy. They take us below the superficial to a happiness founded in those genuine values that put us in touch with God. Our human experience of this happiness may in some cases be unrealized in this world and may have to wait for fulfilment until the 'kingdom of heaven'.

Shortly after the Beatitudes, Matthew gives us the Lord's Prayer. There are three activities to be done in secret in the presence of only our Father in heaven. These are almsgiving, prayer and fasting. This is especially true of prayer. We are to retire to our inner room, perhaps a reference to the inmost room of our own hearts, and there to pray to God as loving Father.

As part of the teaching of Jesus Matthew gives more parables than the other three evangelists. Among those unique to Matthew are the beautiful, brief parables of the treasure hidden in the field and the pearl of great price. Another saying, unique to Matthew and coming from his predilection for community, is 'everybody's favourite' and is quoted by every prayer-group: 'Again I say to you, if two of you agree on earth about anything they ask, it will be done for them by my Father in heaven. For where two or three are gathered in my name, there am I in the midst of them' (18:20).

The Jesus of Matthew's gospel emphasizes responsibility and accountability for one's actions. So, we have the great story of the last judgment in the twenty-fifth chapter. It is both our consolation and our challenge that whatever we do for our brothers or sisters in need, we do for the Lord himself. As with St John, we cannot love the God whom we do not see if we do not love the brother or sister we do see. It is our attitude to the hungry and thirsty, the stranger and the prisoner that is the true test of our love. This is one of the many places where Matthew employs the apocalyptic language current at the time to have Jesus warn about eternal fire, something barely mentioned in the other three gospels.

As we pray with the five great discourses of Jesus in Matthew we come across sayings like, 'You are the salt of the earth ... you are the light of the world' (5:13-14), 'How much more will your heavenly Father give good things to those who ask him' (7:11), 'By their fruits you will know them' (7:20)—just a few examples of the many powerful statements of Christian spirituality that are unique to Matthew's gospel.

The gospels of Matthew and Luke both introduce their readers to Jesus through a genealogy and through two chapters of stories about his infancy that are designed to fire the imagination. A significant difference in the genealogies arises from their intended audiences. Where Luke, writing for Gentiles, traces the line of Jesus backwards to Adam, the universal man, and so to God, Matthew, writing for Jews, begins his ancestry from Abraham, the Father of the Jewish people. Another aspect of Matthew's jewishness is that the father, Joseph, is the key figure in the infancy stories about Jesus, whereas Luke, the evangelist of women, gives the central role to Mary. We tend to think of the Annunciation as a marian event, but in the gospel of Matthew, the birth of Jesus is announced in a dream to Joseph. As Matthew draws on the Old Testament, Joseph, like his namesake in Genesis, becomes the one with whom God communicates frequently through dreams.

The story of the visit of the three wise men from the east leads into the story of the flight into Egypt, so that Jesus the Jew embodies in himself the history of his people in coming out of Egypt. 'Out of Egypt have I called my son' (Matthew 2:15).

In the infancy stories, Luke presents Jesus as the salvation of the peoples. Matthew presents him as God-with-us. As usual, he quotes a fulfilment of the Old Testament, in this case Isaiah 7:14: 'A virgin shall conceive and bear a son and his name shall be called Emmanuel, a name which means God-with-us' (Matthew 1:23). In fact, the tiny preposition 'with' becomes a key theme of Matthew's gospel. The name which Jesus was given in the first chapter is repeated in the very last words of the gospel, showing its importance for the whole. 'Behold I am with you always; yes, to the end of time' (Matthew 28:10). Where Luke has Jesus depart from his disciples in an 'ascension into heaven', in Matthew he simply remains on the mountain *with* them.

The idea of 'being with' is used by Matthew to convey that intimate relationship with Jesus that is so precious to him. It stands out specially at the crucial time of the gospel, as Jesus goes to his death and resurrection. In Mark, Jesus says to the disciples, 'You will all lose faith'. For Matthew this becomes: 'You will all lose faith *in* (*relationship to*) *me*' (26:31). Where Mark goes on to say, 'They came to a place called Gethsemane', Matthew changes this to, 'Jesus came *with them* to a place called Gethsemane'. In Mark, Peter, James and John are told, more than once, to watch. Matthew changes this to watch *with me*.

Matthew has a special interest in personal relationship that is not in the other evangelists. For Mark, Jesus begins his Gethesemane prayer with the address 'Abba, Father' ; for Luke it is 'Father'; for Matthew '*My* Father'. Very consistently then he opens the Lord's Prayer with '*Our* Father', where the equally consistent Luke uses the address 'Father'. Similarly Matthew is interested in family. He alone among the evangelists repeatedly refers to James and John as 'the sons of Zebedee'.

For the Jews, salvation is essentially a community matter. It took a long time for the Old Testament writers to develop the notion of individual responsibility. Matthew sees salvation as coming to groups of people. He obviously quaintly changes the stories in presenting the Gerasene demoniac as *two* demoniacs, and Bartimaeus, the blind man of Jericho, as *two* blind men. In Matthew even the Palm Sunday donkey becomes *two* donkeys, this time, as so often for Matthew, to fulfil an Old Testament prophecy, in this case Zechariah 9:9.

Praying with the gospel of Matthew, we meet a Jesus who is strong and clear in his teaching, who beautifully proclaims the blessings of the kingdom (the Beatitudes), as well as giving firm moral teaching with promises of reward and warnings of punishment. This Jesus wants to be with his people in a relationship that is intimate and personal, and promises that where two or three gather in his name, he is present in their midst. He is with us always, until the end of time.

Praying with Luke

OF THE FOUR GOSPELS, LUKE'S STANDS
out as the one which clearly gives more emphasis to prayer than any
of the others.

First, there is the personal prayer of Jesus himself. Mark has two
references to Jesus's going off alone or to a lonely place to pray. Luke
expands these to five. He does this by introducing the theme of the
prayer of Jesus at the key times in his mission. The revelation of the
Father and of the Spirit at his Baptism takes place when Jesus turns to
prayer after being baptised. It is while Jesus is praying that he turns to
his disciples to ask them the central question of the gospel, 'Who do
you say that I am?' At the Transfiguration Jesus doesn't simply go up
the mountain with the three disciples, but goes up the mountain to
pray. Before choosing his twelve apostles, he spends the whole night
in prayer to God.

Luke not only gives us the example of Jesus at prayer, but also
the most extensive and profound teaching about prayer. A favourite
text with regard to contemplation is Luke's remark that Mary treas-
ured all the events of the infancy of Jesus and pondered them in her
heart. The importance of this verse for contemplating the mystery of
Jesus is emphasized by Luke's writing it after the nativity (2:19) and

repeating it after the finding in the temple (2:51).

From Luke we receive the Lord's Prayer, which is expanded by Matthew into the form we use in our liturgy. Luke gives the great Christian prayer in response to a request from the disciples to be taught how to pray. People who pray it are repeatedly struck by the intimacy evoked by the simple address, 'Father, hallowed be thy name', as compared with the more formal speech of Matthew, 'Our Father, who art in heaven'. Luke then continues in the eleventh chapter to give us the sublime teaching of Jesus about the absolute certainty that all prayer is answered, the fatherhood of God, and the gift of the Holy Spirit every time we pray (11:1-13). In fact, the emphasis on the Holy Spirit is another special feature of Luke's gospel.

Two parables about perseverance in prayer that appear only in Luke are the story of the friend who comes asking for bread in the middle of the night because an unexpected visitor has come (chapter 11) and the widow who badgers the unjust judge until he gives her justice (chapter 18). Also unique to Luke is the story of the pharisee and the publican, with its contrast between spurious and authentic prayer. The tax-collector comes before God, just as he is, with nothing to present but his sin and his need. This, says Jesus, is the kind of prayer that puts a person in touch with God and at rights with God.

Luke and Matthew each give us two chapters of infancy stories about Jesus. Their stories are quite different, with very little in common. Luke tells the stories of the birth of John the Baptist, the annunciation to Mary, the visitation, the birth of Jesus, his naming and circumcision, the presentation in the temple and the finding in the temple. He adds to these his two brief, summary, but important accounts of the hidden life of Jesus, Mary and Joseph at Nazareth, during which Jesus grew to maturity, blessed with God's favour and the gift of wisdom.

The stories are told to enable the reader to contemplate who Jesus is. Where John, in his prologue, gives a philosophical-theological understanding of the Word-made-flesh, Luke appeals directly to our imagination, with very simple, powerful pictures and symbols that prepare an easy entry into our hearts. At his birth the angels announce to the Jewish shepherds, 'This day is born to you a saviour, who is

Christ the Lord'. At the presentation in the awe-inspiring temple of the Lord, Simeon proclaims, 'My eyes have seen your salvation, which you have prepared for all nations to see'.

Luke obviously wishes to teach us that Jesus, from the first moment of his human existence, brings salvation; he does this by appealing not directly to our intelligence, but to our power of contemplation. As we contemplate the scenes we are put into direct, human, personal contact with Jesus as saviour. At the nativity, for instance, we are invited to be like children in the presence of the Christmas crib. The simple, joyful pictures of angels and their song, shepherds and their sheep, and the baby in a manger quickly capture our imagination The scenes themselves draw us into contemplation, like Mary, who 'pondered all these things in her heart' (2:19).

From Luke's infancy narratives the church has taken the two great canticles that conclude its morning prayer and evening prayer every day: the *Benedictus* of Zechariah, and the *Magnificat* of Mary. Also in the liturgy are the other two canticles of Luke, the *Gloria* of the Eucharist and the *Nunc Dimittis* of night prayer. These prayers, like the stories that surround them, have a pervasive lightness and joy, as well as a great strength. The essential message is always the same: God 'has raised up a horn of salvation for us in the house of his servant David' (*Benedictus*); 'my spirit rejoices in God my saviour' (*Magnificat*); 'my eyes have seen your salvation' (*Nunc Dimittis*); and 'Today is born for you a saviour', the message of the angel before the singing of the *Gloria*.

As we take up the gospel of Luke to contemplate the life of Jesus in order to know, love and follow him more truly, we are immediately struck by the strength and beauty of the stories in this gospel. Luke is the great story-teller. The list of stories that appear *only* in his gospel reads like an inventory of everybody's favourites: the annuciation to Mary, the nativity, the sinful woman at Simon's banquet, the good Samaritan, the prodigal and the elder son, the pharisee and the publican, Dives and Lazarus, the ten lepers, Zacchaeus, the repentant robber, the road to Emmaus. The beauty of the crafting of each of these stories, the powerful economy of words, the striking imagery, the accuracy of the expression of the message all combine to help us to contemplate. They make a unique contribution to our putting on more of the mind and heart of Jesus. Luke makes it clear that the Jesus whom we meet in the gospel of Luke is the one who is risen; he is the Lord, a title preferred for him by Luke far more than by the other three gospels.

If we want to pick out one theme of Luke's gospel as being especially dominant, it is the compassion of Jesus, both in his person and in his teaching. This is the gospel of divine mercy. Besides the stories mentioned above, nearly all of which focus on compassion or forgiveness, Luke makes the mercy of Jesus a key theme of the crucifixion, with the incident of the weeping women of Jerusalem, the words of Jesus 'Father forgive them for they do not know what they are doing' and the forgiveness of the dying robber. Repeatedly throughout the gospel we have the phrase 'moved with compassion', as in the stories of the widow of Nain and the good Samaritan.

Another feature unique to Luke is his strong focus on the place of women in the gospel. When we look for mariology, the first gospel we turn to is Luke. Mary is the one who pre-eminently does the will of God, not only in the infancy narratives, but when she appears in his public life. Jesus proclaims, 'My mother and my brothers are those who hear the word of God and do it' (8:21). Luke very cleverly reverses the wording, turning what look likes rejection of Mary in the gospel of Mark into praise for her as the one who is living out her commitment at the annunciation: 'Let it happen to me according to your word' (1:38). Jesus praises his mother in the same way when a woman calls out: 'Blessed is the womb that bore you and the breasts that you sucked' (11:27). He replies, obviously referring to Mary, 'Blessed rather are those who hear the word of God and keep it' (11:29). Mary is the one named by Luke among the many women who gathered with the apostles to pray and await the coming of the Holy Spirit at Pentecost.

There are many women whose stories are told only by Luke: John the Baptist's mother Elizabeth, Anna, the widow of Nain, the sinner at Simon's banquet, Martha and Mary, the woman bent double, the woman who lost the coin, the widow and the unjust judge, the weeping women of Jerusalem.

While having its own special character, referred to above, Luke follows the gospel of Mark, both in basic structure and in reproducing very many of the verses of Mark's gospel. The baptism, the temptations, the feeding of the five thousand, the great question: 'Who do you say that I am?', the Transfiguration, the prophecies of the passion and of resurrection, and the conditions of discipleship are all in place. Quite early in both gospels we reach the turning point, the Transfiguration, with the whole emphasis shifting now to the coming sufferings of Jesus. Luke highlights this in his own special way by proclaiming that immediately after the Transfiguration 'he set his face to go to Jerusalem' (9:51). Over the next eight chapters Luke goes on to relate many parables and some incidents from the life of Jesus, which do not appear in Mark. Throughout all of this Jesus is on his way to Jerusalem to die and rise again.

When Jesus does rise, for Luke there is no return to Galilee, as in the other three. Jesus ascends from Jerusalem. The first part of Luke's writing is now complete. In the Acts of the Apostles he will tell the story of how the new church makes its way from Jerusalem to Rome, always maintaining his emphasis on Jesus as Lord, the all-pervasive presence of the Holy Spirit, and the centrality of prayer.

For Luke in Acts prayer is not a periodic, incidental activity, but it pervades everything the new Christians do. It is the source of their mission. Whatever touches the lives of the disciples is brought to the Lord in prayer. We could take as a summary of Luke's work the dying prayer of Stephen in Acts: 'Stephen, filled with the Holy Spirit, prayed: "Lord Jesus, receive my spirit. Lord, do not hold this sin against them"'.

Prayer is
a Revelation

PRAYING WITH JOHN'S GOSPEL MEANS focusing on the person of Jesus who comes into the world to reveal the Father to us.

Perhaps the most striking thing about John's gospel is its continual and varied use of powerful symbolism. Some of the outstanding themes of this gospel are: eternal life, water (present in every chapter from one to nine, and again in thirteen, nineteen and twenty-one), light and dark, world, work, union, indwelling, the coming of Jesus from God and his return to God through being lifted up. But the key to all of this is that Jesus came into the world to reveal who God is. 'No-one has ever seen God. The only Son, who is into the heart of the Father, has made God known' (1:18). This imparting of knowledge is far more than a satisfaction of the mind's curiosity; it is a knowledge which is life. To know Jesus is to share God's life. 'This is eternal life to know you, the only true God, and Jesus Christ whom you have sent' (17:3).

No-one has ever seen God. In this context the theme of seeing becomes very important for the gospel of John. As he does so often, John imparts a double meaning to the word. It first has the ordinary meaning of seeing, either with the eyes of flesh or the eyes of the

imagination. This is possible not only for those who walked with him
or had a chance meeting with him, but for every Christian in our own
day. In the prologue to the first letter of John the author writes:

> 'Something which has existed from the beginning
> that we have heard,
> that we have seen with our own eyes;
> that we have watched
> and touched with our hands:
> the Word, who is life—
> this is our subject.
> That life was made visible:
> We saw it and are giving our testimony,
> telling you of the eternal life
> which was with the Father and has been made visible to us.
> What we have seen and heard
> we are telling you,
> so that you too may be in union with us,
> as we are in union
> with the Father
> and with his Son Jesus Christ.
> We are writing this to you to make our own joy complete.'
>
> 1 John 1:1-4

This author certainly wrote long after the death of the Lord. He
was writing in the name of the community, some of whose members
had in fact walked with Jesus. In just three verses we have the words
'saw', 'watched' or 'made visible' no fewer than six times. What this
author had done was to contemplate in his prayer the Jesus whose
story had been handed on in the johannine community, so that in this
way he was able to number himself among those who had had truly
'seen' the Lord. Through personal contemplation we are able to do
the same.

For John the word 'see', like the word 'come' takes on the second
meaning of believe into. Notice the preposition 'into'. To believe means
far, far more than to give credence to. Unfortunately, in English the

words are changed to 'believe in', because that is the ordinary way we speak. We can believe in, trust, give credence to any human person. But to 'believe into' Jesus is something different. It is unique. It means to come into living union with the person of Jesus. In the first chapter of the gospel John sets up the importance of the two words 'Come and see' with the invitation of Jesus to the first two disciples. They came and they saw, and they stayed with him (in contemplation) for the rest of that day.

In the twelfth chapter some Greeks at the festival mention to Philip that they would like to *see* Jesus, on the surface a simple human request, but it immediately leads Jesus into a great prayer about his 'hour'. It is only through the hour of his being lifted up, the paschal mystery, that we can really see him by coming to real faith in him. 'When I am lifted up from the earth, then you will know that I am he' (8:28).

Philip is again the one associated with seeing when he requests Jesus at the supper to 'show us the Father'. This gives John the opportunity to state again the whole purpose and fundamental theme of his gospel: 'Philip, the one who sees me sees the Father'.

Contemplation of these rich and powerful symbols teases our minds. We sense levels of meaning that can never be exhausted. Words like 'life', 'water' and 'light' are so basic to all human experience that they evoke countless different associations for different people. Already they lead us deep within even before we move to more religious words like 'eternal life', 'communion' and 'mission'. And standing behind all the words is the majestic, johannine figure of Jesus who speaks with supreme authority of being one with God.

The Jesus of John's gospel sets out to reveal who he is and simultaneously who the Father is. One of John's great techniques for doing this is to have Jesus use the words that God used to Moses at the burning bush: 'I am'. Only in the gospel of John does Jesus proclaim, ' I am ... the Bread of Life, the Good Shepherd, the Gate, the Resurrection and the Life, the Way, the Truth and the Life, the Light of the World, the Vine ...' Each of these words is an invitation to the praying person to enter into the mystery of who Jesus is through contemplation. They become for us favourite images of Jesus. They set up their resonance deep within us, revealing to us who Jesus is, and through him who the Father is.

In the gospel of John, Jesus repeatedly invites people to come to him and to see him. Besides their plain, ordinary meaning the words 'come' and 'see' imply entry into that personal relationship with the Lord that the other gospels call faith and John calls 'believing into him'. This believing establishes a vital, personal union. He and I are truly one. More than that, to be one with Jesus is to be one with the Father. Besides this personal union with the Father and the Son (through the Spirit) there is the communion of all who share this union. Christians are truly one. This is their witness to the world that they are disciples and that the one of whom they are disciples, Jesus, has been sent from the Father. These are the themes of the johannine Lord's Prayer, the high priestly prayer of chapter seventeen of the gospel.

It is through the paschal mystery, which John calls the 'lifting up' of Jesus, that union and communion are established. In the great discourse at the Last Supper, chapters fourteen to sixteen, John is looking back from the perspective of the already glorified Lord and spelling out the richness of the life of personal union with him. In each of these three chapters there is a reference to 'praying in my name'.

Jesus is quoted as saying, 'Up until now you have not asked for anything in my name' (16:24). The meaning of this is that it is only through his glorification that this particular kind of prayer becomes possible. The other characteristic of 'prayer in my name' is that it is infallible. Once in each of the three chapters Jesus declares that whatever we ask the Father in his name will be granted. A pretty important form of prayer then! What does it mean?

In ancient Jewish culture a person's name signified the power and impact of the person. So, to 'pray in my name' means far more than simply adding the words 'through Jesus Christ our Lord' to every prayer. Prayer in the name is prayer arising out of, and attentive to, my personal union with the Lord. Each time Jesus speaks about this prayer he adds, 'Whatever you ask for, you will get it'. This does not mean that I will win the lottery. What I really desire when I pray authentically is to grow in divine life and for all of God's people to grow in that life. I am praying for that greater union and communion which is the coming of the Kingdom. If I happen to pray to win the lottery, it is not that external event which the essence of my prayer, but my acknowledgment of God's sovereignty and my total dependence on God. So, I infallibly grow in union with God with respect to the very thing I was asking for. Perhaps that growth may mean a letting go of a desire to be rich!

When speaking of prayer in his name, Jesus promises the disciples that they will perform even greater works than he himself performed. How can this be? For John there is only one work: the bringing-about of greater union with God. Where the work of Jesus was limited to a very brief time span in a very small part of the world, the work of the disciples—us—is to increase the communion of people with God throughout the world and till the end of time. He prays for us, 'those who come after', that we may be truly one in the Father and the Son, just as the Father is in the Son and the Son is in the Father. Then the world will believe that it was the Father who sent him; the world will be converted, and the union of people with God will be increased.

Our personal union with the Lord is the subject of the famous image of the vine and the branches. We must remain at every step of our way united to the vine, because cut off we are useless. The branch is not merely attached to the vine. The vital sap of the vine is what gives life to every branch. This leads John to develop his great theme of abiding, remaining in or indwelling. We must remain in the Lord if we are to bear the fruit (of further union). The Holy Spirit, who is now promised, will dwell within us.

The Spirit brings the Word, love, peace, knowledge, revelation, life, truth, glory. For the gospel of John these words are all equivalent. He invites us to contemplate them in our prayer and so deepen our union and our abiding. If anyone welcomes the Word and the Spirit, the Father will come, together with Jesus, and they will make their home in that person.

Paul at Prayer

FOR EVERY CHRISTIAN, PAUL, THE apostle, is one of the basic examples of a life of prayer. His whole life is both apostolic and prayerful. He is an apostle; he is a man of prayer; his prayer is apostolic.

It all started when Paul fell to the ground on the road to Damascus and met our Lord, Jesus Christ, the son of that God whom, as a devout pharisee, Paul had always worshipped (see Acts 26:1-23). In this experience he learned two great truths:

—that God is the Father of our Lord, Jesus Christ

—that the Lord Jesus Christ lives in the Christian community and in every Christian. "'Who are you, Lord?" "I am Jesus whom you are persecuting'" (Acts 26:15).

Putting these two truths together, Paul concludes that God is the Father of every Christian. It leads him to the great insight of adoptive sonship or daughtership (see Romans 8:14-17).

The seed of Paul's call (a better word than 'conversion' for what actually happened) was a sudden, unexpected and brief spiritual experience. It is the same in the lives of many of us. We look back to a 'golden moment' when we met the Lord, when he was very close. We tend to over-romanticize the great figures of history. We imagine Paul's call as being dramatic, instantaneous and complete. Rather, he had to live it out, to 'depth' it, to reflect continually on what had happened, in order to grow in that initial relationship with Jesus. Immediately after the Damascus experience, he withdrew to the desert (Galatians 1:17). It was during this time of prayer that his call took root and grew strong.

One thing was very clear to Paul: that his call to be a Christian was a call to be an apostle. He announces himself in the title of his greatest letter as Paul, called-an-apostle (Romans 1:1). His whole identity as a Christian was apostolic. He refers throughout his letters to his prayer for his people, for the infant churches. Among his greatest sufferings he lists 'my anxiety for all the churches' (2 Corinthians 11:28).

On the road to Damascus Paul met Jesus. His whole life, both prayer and apostolate, then becomes a search to know the Lord more intimately. As he tells the story of his call in the great chapter three of Philippians, he is led to reflect that 'all I want is to know Christ and the power of his resurrection, and to share his sufferings, so that I, too, may attain the resurrection from the dead' (Philippians 3:10). He doesn't seek to know about Jesus, but to go on deepening the heart knowledge of personal relationship. The gift received on the Damascus road is not something static, once and for all. It demands a continual growth and depthing through a life of prayer in response to grace. 'Not that I have already obtained this or am already perfect; but I press on to make it my own, because Christ Jesus has made me his own' (Philippians 3:12).

Paul declares that even if he knew Christ 'from a human point of view', such knowledge would have been as nothing compared to the knowledge of the risen Lord gained through prayer in response to the new creation of grace (2 Corinthians 5:16). Where is the Christ Paul is searching for? He is right in the heart of Paul. 'For me, to live is Christ' (Philippians 1:21). 'I live, now not I, but Christ lives in me' (Galatians 2:20).

Again, in Galatians chapter one, Paul is reflecting on the experience of his call. 'He who had set me apart before I was born, and had called me through his grace, was pleased to reveal his Son in me, in order that I might preach him to the Gentiles' (Galatians 1:15-16). The determining factors for the style of Paul's prayer are that Jesus is in him and that he must be apostolic. Christ is revealed to him; he is revealed through him; he is always with him, but primarily Christ is *in* him.

In his greatest chapter on the Resurrection, 1 Corinthians 15, Paul again gives his reflections on his road to Damascus call. It is sheer grace: 'Last of all, as to one untimely born, he appeared to me' (v.8). 'By the grace of God, I am what I am, and his grace towards me was not in vain. On the contrary, I worked harder than any, though it was not I, but the grace of God in me' (vv. 10-11). Once again prayer (response to the the grace of God) and apostolate (hard work in union with that grace) are inseparably linked, as two sides of the same coin.

Paul provides every Christian with a model of prayer life. It is a continuing drawing on the grace of God's call, our Baptism, in order to be on mission for the coming of the Kingdom. Everything we do in our lives gives expression to the Christ-life within.

Again and again in the letters Paul tells the stories of his adventures in spreading the Kingdom throughout the Mediterranean. Every detail of every story is related to the presence of the risen Lord who journeys with him every step of the way. We must always remember 'God's inexpressible gift' (2 Corinthians 9:15) and 'press on to make it our own' (Philippians 3:12). The life of the Spirit that Paul writes about in Romans 8 and Galatians 4 is given to all in Baptism. The Spirit in us makes us adoptive children of God, and cries, 'Abba! Father!' (Romans 8:15, Galatians 4:6).

A life of mystical union is given to every Christian; each of us is able to join in the life of mystical prayer, about which Paul was writing, not in abstract theology but in terms of his own experience, when he wrote, 'Likewise the Spirit helps us in our weakness; for we do not know how to pray as we ought, but the Spirit himself intercedes for us with sighs too deep for words. And he who searches the hearts of men knows what is the mind of the Spirit, because the Spirit intercedes for the saints according to the will of God' (Romans 8:26-27).

Eternally
Grateful

'REJOICE ALWAYS; PRAY WITHOUT ceasing; give thanks in everything; for this is the will of God for you in Christ Jesus' (1 Thessalonians 5:16-18).

This is a very important text from St Paul's letters. In it he gives the classic summary of his constantly repeated teaching about Christian prayer. That teaching is that the Christian ought to have three fundamental life attitudes: prayer, thanks and joy. Each time he uses these three, Paul adds to each one expressions like 'always', 'constantly', 'without ceasing', 'in all things', 'in every situation'.

The text has led many Christians over the centuries to ask: How is it possible to pray always?

One of the classic answers has been that of the 'Jesus prayer'. In fact, in *The Way of the Pilgrim* 1 Thessalonians 5:17 is used as the rationale for repeating thousands of times a day 'Jesus Christ, Son of God, have mercy upon me'. While the Jesus prayer is a wonderful way of praying and has led many to enter deeply into the heart, the exegesis of 1 Thessalonians 5:17 is not correct. What Paul is exhorting the people to are three fundamental *attitudes of heart*. 'Pray without ceasing' really means 'Be in a constant state of Prayer, of relationship with God'. The Christian is to be a prayerful, joyful, thankful person, whether saying prayers, working, or recreating.

'This is the will of God for you in Christ Jesus' is a significant reflection on this state of prayer. It is God's will that initiates, that gifts us with a share in divine life, and does so through our union with Christ. This union is the basic theme of Paul's letters. Through the gift of union with Christ, through Baptism, the Christian is put into right relationship with God. Prayer, joy and thanksgiving are gifts of God to be constantly responded to in all our living.

By the very fact of our creation our attitude must be one of *constant* prayer. We do not *start* to pray; we simply get in touch with the gift of the state of prayer implanted in us by the creator. Our relationship with God truly 'comes alive'.

What sort of prayer is appropriate to a creature in the presence of its creator? One of thanksgiving. We are thankful for the gift of life. In Paul's thinking we are to be especially grateful for the gift of the life of Christ in us. This is what he was referring to when he wrote, 'Thanks be to God for his inexpressible gift' (2 Corinthians 9:15).

It is humanly impossible to be thankful and miserable at the same time. Try standing in front of a mirror; pull a sour face, and say in a depressed voice, 'Thank you very much'. It doesn't work! Saying 'Thanks' makes us smile. As the modern saying has it, 'We are Easter people'. As Christians we are called to witness to the world the joy of our faith in the risen Lord. This is far more than having a bright personality or an optimistic outlook on life. It is an attitude of heart rising from faith, hope and love and flowing over into the whole person.

The best known of Paul's trilogies of prayer, joy and thanks is the one in the letter to the Philippians: 'Rejoice in the Lord always; again I say rejoice … in everything by prayer and supplication with thanksgiving let your requests be known to God' (Philippians 4:4-6). In the same letter Paul has the very affectionate, personal introduction: 'I thank my God each time I remember you, always, in every prayer for you, making my prayer with joy' (Philippians 1:3-4). Some Christians today follow this example in speaking and writing to one another with similar words. The letters of Paul are full of them. Try searching them out. To conclude with just two very personal ones, to

Timothy and to Philemon, 'I thank God when I remember you constantly in my prayers. As I remember your tears, I long night and day to see you, so that I may be filled with joy' (2 Timothy 1:3). 'I thank my God always when I remember you in my prayers. I have derived much joy and comfort from your love' (Philemon 4-7).

The Heights
and the
Depths

that they have two main types of prayer experience. On the one hand there are times of peace, joy, wonder, exhilaration. On the other hand there is darkness, struggle, turmoil and near-despair. These kinds of experience are reported by Teresa, Julian of Norwich, Ignatius, John of the Cross and innumerable Christians of our day. The first Christian to give an account of this almost universal experience was St Paul.

Paul's credentials as an apostle were often under attack from his rivals; so he needed to defend himself. In the second letter to the Corinthians he is doing this kind of 'boasting', calling on a quotation from Jeremiah about 'boasting in the Lord' (Jeremiah 9:24). This leads him to give an account in chapter 12 of two different kinds of experience in prayer.

Paul calls his positive, 'wonderful' experience a 'vision' or 'revelation'. Already he is beginning to hint that it is impossible to put exact words on such an experience. In our own times it is very common for people reporting a wonderful prayer experience to say things like 'Of course, I haven't had any visions, but ...' There is no special value in being able or unable to use the word 'vision' or any similar word. Nor is there any way of 'measuring' my experience against someone else's. I do not have to say, 'Of course, my experience wasn't as great as the one Paul describes in 2 Corinthians 12'. All I need to do and must do is humbly acknowledge the reality of the Lord's personal gift to me.

Paul goes on to say he was 'caught up into paradise'. This does not mean 'heaven', the state of everlasting bliss. Otherwise he couldn't have returned to earth! All that Paul is claiming is a mystical experience of extreme happiness, the 'exhilaration' referred to above. There has been a tradition among Christian spiritual writers to single out the meeting of Moses with God and the experience Paul describes here as the 'greatest' mystical experiences ever reported. It is a fruitless task to compare such experiences. By the very nature of the case evidence is lacking. Paul reports that he heard things that cannot be told, that a human being may not utter. The reason why we may not utter such things is simply that they are beyond putting into words. Similarly, very many people today have wonderful experiences in prayer that truly merit the name 'mystical'.

Another characteristic of Paul's report, one common to many— I would even say most—persons of prayer is the accurate memory involved. The experience he writes about had happened fourteen years earlier. Once we have met the Lord in a way like this, we can never forget. It can dominate our relationship with him. Quite rightly our spiritual life becomes a continual drawing upon the grace initially given in that one encounter. Reflection on Paul's account of his experience should encourage us to search our own memory for times of special closeness to the Lord. If I have no such memories, then I can be encouraged to expect some experience of this kind in the future!

After telling about his 'vision', Paul very wisely goes on immediately to report a struggle in prayer—something that perhaps we find far more common than wonderful, positive experience. This struggle concerned a 'thorn in the flesh'. There is no way of knowing what this phrase implies, except that it was some obstacle to Paul's apostolate. Many scripture scholars see it as a reference to a physical handicap or illness, such as that referred to in Galatians 4:12, 'You know it was because of a bodily ailment that I preached the gospel to you at first', and perhaps also in 2 Corinthians 1:8, 'For we do not want you to be ignorant, brethren, of the affliction we experienced in Asia; for we were so utterly, unbearably crushed that we despaired of life itself'.

As in Matthew's account of Jesus praying in Gethsemane, Paul prays 'three times'. This is a symbolic phrase, meaning prolonged and earnest prayer. Also, like Jesus, Paul does not receive the direct answer to prayer which he started out seeking. The thorn in the flesh must remain. Paul, again like Jesus, receives multiple answers to his prayer. He receives the conviction that the Lord's strength is enough to keep him going, and that that strength is at its best when he himself feels most weak. He receives a new joy and a new sense of the Lord's presence. There is no doubt that Paul found this kind of prayer a real struggle. The fruit did not become immediately or easily obvious to him. He sees this kind of prayer as the Lord's gift to him to 'keep me from becoming too elated'.

We are in good company when we experience struggle, weakness and difficulty in prayer. When we do, we must avoid any temptation to wallow in it. The experience of scaling the heights is also available to us, as well as that of plumbing the depths. All that is required is that we be present and available to the Lord in whatever way he wishes to come to us.

The Lord's
Prayer

JESUS WAS IN A CERTAIN PLACE PRAYING,
and when he finished, one of his disciples said to him, 'Lord, teach us
to pray, as John taught his disciples'. And he said to them, 'When you
pray, say:

> Father,
> Hallowed be thy name.
> Thy kingdom come.
> Give us each day our daily bread;
> And forgive us our sins; for we ourselves
> forgive everyone who is indebted to us
> And save us in the time of trial.'
>
> Luke 11:1-4

Here we have the Lord's Prayer as presented by Jesus in response
to the disciples' request to be taught how to pray.

We notice first that this version in Luke's gospel is shorter than
the one we are used to, from the gospel of Matthew. It is shorter not
because Luke has omitted anything, but because Matthew has expanded
the prayer to give it more balance and rhythm for liturgical recitation.

So, if the actual words of Jesus are what we are looking for, we would do better to use the Lord's Prayer from Luke rather than from Matthew. Strictly, it should not be called the 'Our Father'; the word 'our' is not included; it is the Lord's Prayer.

It can be a very helpful prayer exercise to try saying the Lord's Prayer from Luke's gospel several times. Many people find that by doing this they experience a greater intimacy in using the simple, direct address 'Father' rather than the more formal 'Our Father, who art in heaven'.

In the prayer, after the address, there are two different groups of petitions, which are referred to as the 'thou petitions' and the 'we petitions'. Luke has two of the former and three of the latter. Matthew introduces balance by adding a third 'thou' petition, 'Thy will be done'.

Hallowed be thy name. There is far more to this prayer than exclaiming, 'Praise the Lord', or asking that people will express reverence for the name of God. The modern translation, 'May your name be held holy', is an error. The petition really asks that God's name be made holy. What does this mean? For the Jews the name was the life of the person. Moreover, the Jews had the custom of putting a request for God to act into the passive. It is more reverent than simply telling God to do something. What the petition means is fact is 'Father, make your life holy'.

But God's life is eternally, infinitely holy in Godself. God makes that life holy in God's people by sharing that life with us more fully. As Evelyn Underhill puts it, 'Our response to each experience that God puts in our path, from the greatest disclosure of beauty to the smallest appeal to love, from perfect happiness to utmost grief, will either hallow or not hallow God's name'.

The gospel of John does not give us the Lord's Prayer in a form close to that of Luke or Matthew, but in a much longer form, the whole of John's seventeenth chapter. This chapter is dominated by the address, 'Father', by 'Glorify your name' and by 'Keep them safe from trial'. At the start of this great prayer John spells out for us the real meaning of 'Hallowed be thy name': 'Father, glorify your Son, so that your Son may glorify you, and through the power over all humankind you have give to him, let him *give eternal life* to all those you have entrusted to him' (John 17:1-2).

The next petition means the same thing. The Kingdom of God comes when God lives and rules in the hearts of God's people. The 'rule' in this kingdom is from within, from the Spirit who is Love and Life. The prayer is once again that the Father share as fully as possible his life with us, his People. So, our first two petitions are a request for a fuller share of divine life through communion with God. Anthony Bloom neatly brings out the meaning of these first two petitions: 'It is not our words or our gestures that give glory to the name of God, it is our being God's kingdom, which is the radiance and glory of our maker and our saviour'. As we shall see later, the third petition of Matthew means precisely the same thing. The fundamental cry goes up from the human heart to the Father for more profound communion.

It is not surprising when we turn to the three 'we petitions' to find that once again we are dealing in the Lord's prayer with the most fundamental aspects of human life: the bread of life, forgiveness and salvation.

The petition for daily bread does not seem to be a prayer for our three meals a day. A tradition of exegesis going right back to St Jerome in the fourth century sees this as a petition for the food of our life's journey into the great tomorrow of the Lord. We are asking for the bread for this journey, principally the Eucharist. If our prayer is genuine, then we will be moved to spend ourselves in working to bring about the alleviation of the hunger of our starving brothers and sisters. In this sense the prayer will lead to the supplying of our 'ordinary' bread.

We pray for forgiveness, not because the Lord needs to be reminded to forgive, but because we need to open our hearts to accept that forgiveness. This opening up is shown especially in our forgiving those who have offended us. 'For we ourselves forgive ...' As we ask for God's grace we declare our willingness to forgive others. The unforgiving cannot receive God's forgiveness, however much God wishes to bestow it. It is not as if we forgive and then God forgives. Rather, the grace of forgiveness that we receive is the same grace that empowers us to forgive. We become a channel to others of the Lord's forgiveness.

The Lord's prayer, as Luke gives it, ends very abruptly: 'Save us in the time of trial'. We are used to saying 'Lead us not into temptation'. People sometimes puzzle over the words 'lead us not'. Isn't it unthinkable that God would bring us into a situation of evil? Sadly, the great trial or testing is inevitable, and the words 'lead us not' are simply asking God not to allow us to face a trial in which we will succumb, or, in other words, to save us in the time of trial. The word 'temptation' is really a poor translation of the original Greek. We are not concerned here about about a series of enticements to do wrong. It is a matter of that great, global struggle between good and evil in which we are all inevitably involved. In this conflict our faith, like that of the disciples in Gethsemane, is fragile. We ask the Lord not to put us to the test, a nice way of saying that we know we must be tested, but, please, God, keep us safe in the time of trial.

Luke's ending is striking. Without the balancing phrase 'but deliver us from evil' we are left dangling, surprised, alerted. We are made aware of the urgency of this prayer. Good and evil are locked in fierce combat; every one of us is caught up in this struggle, but we are in danger of not noticing it!

The gospels and Paul's letters frequently urge us to stay awake and be watchful, that is, to be alert and aware. We need to watch in order to remain faithful in the face of the onslaught of the powerful forces of evil. The first letter of Peter (5:10) emphasizes this urgency with the words 'Be on the watch [stay awake]. Your enemy the devil prowls around like a roaring lion, seeking someone to devour'.

The
'Our Father'

WHEN WE TURN TO THE 'OUR FATHER' in Matthew, we are on familiar ground. Notice how Matthew adds the personal pronoun 'our' to Luke's address to the Father. The evangelists are very consistent. Matthew is the one who most favours using personal pronouns to express intimate relationship and community. In the gospel of Matthew, when Jesus prays in Gethsemane, he addresses God as 'My Father'. For Luke on both occasions the address is simply 'Father'.

Matthew balances the address, 'Our Father', with the formal phrase 'who art in heaven'. He neatly completes the next section of the prayer, the three 'thou' petitions, with the same phrase 'on earth as it is in heaven'. In the structure of the prayer this phrase applies to all three petitions, not just to 'Thy will be done'. Once again Matthew is conscious of balance when he adds the third 'thou' petition for God's will to be done, matching the three 'we' petitions that will come after.

Unfortunately many Christians have grown up in a tradition which associates the will of God primarily with the disastrous happenings of life. The true meaning is the opposite. God wills us to have life to the full. St Paul gives a 'definition' of God's will in 1 Thessalonians 4:13 when he writes, 'This is the will of God, your sanctifying' . Paul is referring not just to the end product, 'sanctification', but to the whole process by which God shares God's life and holiness with us.

So, this is what we are asking for when we pray 'Thy will be done'. When we try to pray this prayer in the face of the trials and difficulties of our life, what is required of us is not a superficial, grudging submission to the will of God who is stronger and more knowing than I am, but a profound, peaceful acceptance. As in the case of Jesus in Gethsemane, it may require a long and intense time of prayer to come to that state of gracefully and peacefully saying a profound 'Yes' to God's will that is expressive of deep union and genuine acceptance.

The petition 'Thy will be done' means the same as 'Hallowed be thy name' and 'Thy kingdom come'. The three are simply different wordings of the same prayer. This being so, the phrase 'on earth as it is in heaven' belongs with all three. Perhaps this is a corrective for us to an old idea that God's will being done on earth as in heaven was really a matter of perfect law and order. The gospel message is less one of law and order than one of life and love—even in the midst of the chaos which must always be associated with being truly human.

In the petition for our daily bread Matthew adheres to the urgency of *this* day, rather than Luke's more expansive 'each day'. In this Matthew is probably being more faithful to the original Aramaic wording of the prayer.

People sometimes complain about not being able to say the Our Father because of the difficulty involved in the prayer for forgiveness. The stumbling-block for them is the little word 'as' in the phrase 'as we forgive those who have sinned against us'. This little conjunction can imply degree or cause or simultaneity of time, or *as* here, it can be a simple link word, which can be omitted without affecting the meaning. Yes, it would be absurd to ask the Father to forgive us in the same measure in which we forgive! Rather, our prayer for forgiveness reminds us of our need to forgive our brother and sister if we are to receive the Lord's forgiveness; moreover, it helps us to make that act of forgiving. Our human forgiving is always inadequate, and each time we say the prayer we are asking for the grace to be more genuinely forgiving.

In the last petition Matthew avoids the abrupt, staccato ending of Luke by adding the phrase 'but deliver us from evil' (or 'the evil one'; the original Greek is open to both translations.) This balances the sentence nicely in parallel with the two previous petitions, and makes the prayer flow rhythmically for recitation by a group. The 'Our Father', the Lord's Prayer for Matthew is preferable for formal, group prayer; the 'Father', the Lord's Prayer for Luke is more intimate for personal prayer.

Children
of God

WE HAVE LOOKED AT THE MEANING OF the words in two versions of the Lord's Prayer: Luke's and Matthew's. We now look a little deeper—into the meaning behind the meanings. The Lord's Prayer has that title because it is the prayer given to his people by Jesus himself. But our primary interest is not in trying to recapture the actual words as Jesus spoke them. This would be impossible.

Not only is this not a cause for concern, but it can even help us capture the true meaning of the prayer. Its importance does not lie in the fact that we use the *words* our Saviour gave us. For one thing, we should all take the trouble to learn a little of the Aramaic language if it was the exact reproduction of the Lord's words that gave the prayer its supreme importance. In fact it is in exact opposition to this kind of thinking that Matthew gives us the prayer. Jesus tells his disciples not to be like the pagans, who thought that by repeating a lot of the right words in prayer formulas they could get through to their gods (Matthew 6:7).

Jesus urges us to pray for God to accomplish God's will in bringing about the coming of the Kingdom by making God's name holy. Dietrich Bonhoeffer sums it up accurately: 'God's name, God's kingdom, God's will must be the primary object of Christian prayer. Of course, it is not as if God needed our prayers, but they are the means by which the disciples become partakers in the heavenly treasures for which they pray. Furthermore, God uses their prayers to hasten the coming of the end.' In the second set of three petitions we are to pray for the bread of life, forgiveness of sin, and the preservation of our faith against the onslaught of evil.

Yet we still haven't touched the essence of this prayer. That essence is really a new relationship with God. Jesus authorizes us to pray as adopted children of his Father through the power of the Spirit living in us. The Spirit cries out in our hearts, 'Abba! Father!' (Romans ch. 8, Galatians ch. 4), and perhaps also, 'Imma! Mother!' Abba and Imma are the intimate names from the Aramaic language that people call their father and mother. However, the essence of this prayer is not just a new intimate word, but a real, infinitely more intimate *relationship*.

Jesus came to reveal to us a new relationship with God. We relate to God as Father in the same way that he does. This relationship is given through the indwelling of the Spirit of the risen Lord. As we have already seen with the sign of the Cross, we are enabled to pray from within the life of the Trinity. God is not a long way off, in a remote heaven. Jesus is not someone who lived a long time ago. God is here; Jesus is now.

When we pray the Lord's Prayer, we pray not in the words our Saviour gave us, but in the *Way* he gave us. Jesus always prays to God by the address 'Father'. The sole exception in the gospels is Mark 15:34 (repeated in Matthew 27:46): 'My God, my God, why have you forsaken me?' Yet, this is not a real exception. Mark was simply drawing attention to the fact that Jesus died with Psalm 22 on his lips; the verse quoted is the opening verse of that psalm.

Jesus always called God 'Father' by virtue of the unique relationship proper to him as *the* Son of God. We now share in that relationship. The Lord's Prayer is the celebration of our life in Christ, our sonship or daughtership of the Father, the gift to us of the Holy Spirit. It is the prayer of our Baptism. Because of this it is especially a eucharistic prayer. Hence its place in our liturgy before Holy Communion.

Because it is the prayer of our Baptism, it has a proper place in the celebration of every Christian sacrament.

It is no wonder that St Teresa of Avila finds in the Lord's Prayer the height of mysticism. She writes in *The Way of Perfection*:

'One day a sister came to me in great distress because she did not know how to make mental prayer, nor could she contemplate, but was only able to pray vocally. I questioned her and found that she enjoyed pure contemplation while saying the Lord's Prayer, and that God had raised her to union with himself. This was evidenced by her conduct, for she lived so holy a life that I thanked God for it, and even envied such vocal prayer.'

St Luke gives us the Lord's Prayer in the context of the gospels' greatest teaching on prayer (Luke 11:1-13). The paragraph ends with the words, 'How much more will your heavenly Father give the Holy Spirit to those who ask him'. The whole passage is a proclamation of the totally loving fatherhood of God. Whenever we pray, what we really desire from God is the gift of the Holy Spirit. This is the fruit of the Lord's Prayer: that the praying person be more fully possessed by the Holy Spirit, have more of the mind and heart of Christ, and be more truly a child of the Father. The Lord's Prayer, then, is not just the greatest Christian prayer, but in a true sense it is the *only* Christian prayer.

Jesus
Man of
Prayer

CATHOLICS WHO WERE EDUCATED PRIOR
to Vatican II were well taught that Jesus is God, and that we, as creatures, ought to be in the habit of addressing our prayers to him. It
didn't sit so comfortably with us that Jesus was a man who prayed to
God. True, we were well aware of the agony in the garden and the
great high priestly prayer of John 17, but we thought of Jesus far more
as the one to whom we pray, rather than as one who prayed like us.
Because he did pray like us, Jesus is our greatest model for a life of
prayer, and it is well worth our while looking into the gospels to learn
something about how he did pray.

One excellent way of approaching the gospels would be to read
them so as to allow them to remind us of Jesus, the man of prayer.

It is certainly clear that his whole life is a prayer. All his attitudes
to life are dominated by awareness, openness and response to the presence of God. In the gospel of John, for example, Jesus never tires of
speaking about his Father, about his mission to 'do the will of him
who sent me'. Apart from this his life would have no meaning.

In the gospels of Matthew, Mark and Luke every person, every thing, every event provides an occasion for Jesus to be aware of God at work in our world. Fishing, boating, farming, weddings, journeys, merchants, kings, lepers, children, the blind, the sick, beggars, men and women all speak to Jesus of the God who is in every human situation. So everything he experiences can become the source of a parable, a story about God's action in the lives of people.

Jesus is pre-eminently, always, in every detail of his life a man of Prayer, that profound attitude of the human heart in the presence of God.

Jesus is truly and fully human. If we take this statement seriously, we must believe that, in order to be the kind of person described above, he, like us, had to spend time alone with his God, to develop and deepen his relationship with God. Jesus was not exempt from the human need for painstaking and often difficult attempts to get in touch with God.

Each of the four gospels tells us something about the personal prayer life of Jesus. Like the prayer life of any of us, it is too personal and too far beyond words for much to be written about it. However, one thing is certainly clear: Jesus often spent time in formal prayer.

Mark mentions on three different occasions that Jesus withdrew from the presence of people in order to pray. Matthew mentions this only twice, but in chapter 11 he gives us a direct report of a prayer that Jesus offered: 'I bless you, Father, Lord of heaven and earth, for hiding these things from the learned and the clever and revealing them to little children. Yes, Father, for that is what it pleased you to do' (11:25-26). This prayer appears also in Luke 10:20-21.

Apart from Gethsemane, closely linked to the prayers of John chapters 12 and 17, there are just four other direct reports of a prayer of Jesus. The first is by John, just before the raising of Lazarus. Jesus prays: 'Father, I thank you for hearing my prayer. I know that you always hear me, but I say this for the sake of those standing around, so that they may believe it was you who sent me' (John 11:41-42). Then Jesus prays on the cross. For Mark, followed by Matthew, it is, 'My God, my God, why have you forsaken me?' (Psalm 22); for Luke, 'Father forgive them, for they know not what they do', and 'Into your hands I commend my spirit'.

When we turn to the gospel of Luke, we have the one among the four in which prayer is most explicitly a theme. Not only does Luke give us in its fullest form the teaching of Jesus about prayer, connected to the Lord's Prayer (11:1-13), but he expands from Mark's three to six the number of times that Jesus goes off alone to pray. In one text he puts it very strongly: ' Great crowds gathered to hear him and to be healed of their illnesses; but he would often withdraw to the wilderness and pray' (5:15-16). Occasionally Jesus took his disciples with him for a time of prayer apart from the crowds, but it was his custom to go off alone to pray.

Jesus withdraws to pray not only as a matter of habit, but very specially on important occasions. The most important of these, which we will reflect on later, is, of course, his prayer before his death and resurrection. In the gospel of Matthew, Jesus hears the news of the death of John the Baptist, and, obviously in deep grief, 'he withdrew to a lonely place apart'. Luke mentions that before choosing the twelve apostles Jesus 'spent the whole night in continuous prayer to God'. Luke makes a special point of setting each of the key gospel events in the context of Jesus's prayer. He does this not only with the choosing of the twelve, but with the Baptism, Peter's profession of faith and the Transfiguration.

Jesus, the man who prayed to God, gives us our model, not only of how to deal with grief or the making of important decisions, but of our need to withdraw at times from our busy-ness to pray alone. This is the foundation for him as well as for us for developing that continuous, profound attitude of heart in God's presence which truly makes life worth living.

Thy Will
Be Done

THE BEST MODEL OF PRAYER FOR A
Christian is given to us in the scriptural accounts of Jesus at prayer
immediately before his arrest and crucifixion. We have been accus-
tomed to summing up these different accounts under the title of 'the
agony in the garden'. It is interesting to note that there are six different versions of this prayer of Jesus: one in each of the gospels of Mark
(14:32-42), Matthew (26:36-46) and Luke (22:39-46), two in John
(12:27-28 and ch. 17), and one in the letter to the Hebrews (5:7-10).

We should not be surprised to learn that there is a great richness
for our personal prayer life in examining each of these accounts—a
richness far greater than is contained in the popular interpretation of
these texts. So we will look closely at these different versions of Jesus-
at-prayer, commencing with the gospel of Mark. We begin with Mark
because it is the earliest of the six accounts. Matthew, in particular,
depends very directly on Mark. He wrote his version of Jesus in
Gethsemane with Mark's account in front of him.

Here we are considering verses 26 to 42 of chapter 14 of Mark's
gospel.

The importance of the first two verses is that they give us the
context for the Gethsemane prayer. As he makes his way out of Jeru-

salem with his disciples on the short walk to the Mount of Olives, Jesus is preoccupied with their coming loss of faith, their scattering or defection. This leads him to quote from the Old Testament: 'I will strike the shepherd and the sheep will be scattered'. It is in the light of this that he will pray. His prayer will be not so much for himself—the shepherd—but especially for them—the sheep. As in John 17, where Jesus prays immediately after warning the disciples that they will all be scattered (16:32), so in Mark and Matthew the prayer of Jesus is that they do not scatter, that they remain in communion.

This moment, his 'hour', is the climax of the mission of Jesus. The global struggle between good and evil is at its most intense. It appears, especially now from their falling asleep, that the disciples are unable to watch, that they will give up in the face of this great testing. Hence the exhortation of Jesus in Mark, Matthew and Luke: 'Watch and pray that you do not succumb in the time of trial'. When they do give up and scatter, the budding Christian community will seem to be finished and the mission of Jesus to fail.

Very many courageous people in the course of history have faced death fearlessly. Yet Mark describes the emotional state of Jesus at this time in very strong words. As the New Jerusalem Bible translates them: 'He began to feel terror and anguish'. It is not so much the act of dying that causes this terror in Jesus, but the fact that his mission would apparently fail. Here he was, sent by the Father to bring about the kingdom of love, peace and justice. After all the striving of his public ministry, his hopes for that kingdom rested in this small band of followers, and they were about to give up. Our minds cannot cope with the horror of this. In fact, so great was the distress of Jesus according to Mark that he was stumbling on the ground.

This setting for the prayer of Jesus underlines his humanness and the need he has for prolonged prayer to come to terms with grief or impending disaster in his life. He cannot simply 'switch over', as we could be tempted to imagine, to his habitual attitude of peace in always doing what was pleasing to his Father. He is faced with a new and unheard-of situation—the disbanding of his disciples, their loss of faith, the failure of his unique mission. In the face of this he must go through the struggle involved in the kind and the length of prayer that will bring him through to a hard-won peace and the ability to say from the heart with conviction, 'Thy will be done'.

The final state of adherence of Jesus to the will of the Father will not be in a general sense ('I always give the Father a blank cheque'), but in accepting the real disaster that is about to happen (' I know that I must now die, that the community will be disbanded and evil seem to triumph, but, Father, I leave it all in your hands. Your will be done').

What happens to the disciples while Jesus prays? He says to eight of them (v. 32), 'Sit here while I pray'. He takes Peter, James and John a little further, then says to them, 'Stay here and watch' (v. 34). It would be difficult to exaggerate the importance of this instruction, the need for 'watching' in the Christian life. There is no suggestion whatever that Jesus is looking to the disciples to back him up in prayer. On the contrary he will pray for them. Watching is an extremely important concept for the early Christian communities. They recognized how fragile the seed of faith is, and the need to be constantly alert to guard it from the evil spirit seeking to pluck it from the heart.

There is a great struggle going on between good and evil, and the front-line runs right through the heart of every Christian. We need to be aware, to watch, to be on our guard. Otherwise, as Luke puts it in the parable of the sower (8:13), 'In time of temptation, they apostasize [lose their faith]. The word 'temptation' means the same here as at the end of the Lord's Prayer—the great, cosmic struggle between good and evil. The moment of Gethsemane and the Lord's Passion is the greatest manifestation of this struggle, and the disciples are caught in the midst of it. How important that they watch, and be aware!

The classic text for the early Christians about the need to watch comes from the first letter of Peter (5:8): 'Be on the watch. Your enemy the devil is prowling around like a roaring lion, seeking someone to devour'. How do the disciples of Jesus cope with this need to be on the watch?

The word 'Gethsemane' literally means 'oil-press'. Located as it is at the foot of the Mount of Olives, it is quite likely a genuinely geographical name. Mark certainly intends to draw the reader's attention to the symbolic crushing that Jesus must undergo in this place. We reached the point where Jesus, seized with sudden terror and anguish, left the disciples to sit and to watch while he prayed. He was so distressed that he was stumbling (this is the tense that Mark uses) on the ground.

Jesus prayed that, if it were possible, the hour might pass him by. The word 'hour' refers here to the time of handing over into the hands of sinners (v. 41). Jesus knows for sure that this is about to happen, but he really wants it not to happen. The only qualification he adds to the prayer is 'if it be possible'. Mark then reports the prayer of Jesus in direct speech. Here he introduces the intimate family address 'Abba'. This is the only place in the four gospels where it is used. This word has played a prominent place in modern spirituality. In Romans 8 and Galatians 4, Paul uses it for the prayer of the Spirit in the heart of the Christian. It suggests a new depth and tender intimacy in the relationship of Jesus and of the Christian to the Father.

Jesus began this prayer by telling the Father that everything is possible for him. He now asks for the cup, the symbol of the dark side of his sacrifice, his death and the disciples' desertion, to be removed. The qualification he adds is 'nevertheless, thy will be done'. Though he has not yet reached serene, profound adherence to God's will concerning the coming events, the movement is in that direction. It is much more than the grudging sort of 'resignation to God's will' that has unfortunately been prominent in much of our past piety and preaching.

Why does Jesus leave his prayer and return to his disciples? This question is of supreme importance. It is not because he needs to break off his struggle and look for support. As the shepherd he is concerned for them, and he shows this concern both in his prayer and in his coming to check out how they are getting on. Conscious of their neediness, he returns to them to see if they are all right, if they are able to 'watch'. In fact they are doing the opposite—sleeping. Jesus does not pray in a separate 'spiritual' world divorced from the events of this earth. What is happening to his disciples will help his prayer to develop. Addressing them, he now adds the word 'pray' to his original instruction to watch, and he tells them exactly what they must pray for: that they do not succumb in the time of trial—enter into temptation—the last petition of the Lord's Prayer.

Immediately after the words of Jesus, 'The spirit is willing, but the flesh is weak', Mark reports that Jesus went away and prayed saying the same words. Mark probably intends to convey that Jesus, in his role as shepherd caring for the flock, takes back to his prayer the weakness of the disciples. 'Father, their spirit is willing, but their flesh is weak.' If this is so, it emphasizes that the prayer of Jesus, like all authentic prayer, takes into account the real, significant events affecting the coming of the Kingdom. The answer to the prayer will then be the tranformation of the praying person with regard to those events. This is precisely what happens to Jesus.

The change is gradual. After the second time of prayer Jesus comes and finds them sleeping again. Mark does not mention that Jesus prayed a third time, but implies it by saying that he came back to the disciples a third time. The idea of praying three times is a literary convention to convey that the prayer is long and earnest. The movement back and forth from the Father to the disciples also underlines that there is a double dialogue going on for Jesus. The change in him comes about gradually, through bringing to the Father in prayer the changing circumstances of the world of the disciples, their deeper and deeper lack of awareness and failure to watch.

There is certainly a real and striking change in Jesus: from the state of sudden terror and anguish, to the peace with which he says, 'Rise, let us go. My betrayer is at hand'. This peace stays with him throughout his Passion.

Finally, it would be difficult to read Mark's account of Gethsemane attentively without noticing the centrality of the Lord's Prayer. That prayer has three parts: the address to the Father, the 'thou' petitions and the 'we' petitions. Each is represented in the Gethsemane prayer. 'Father, thy will be done. Lead us not into temptation.' The Lord's Prayer, which puts us in touch with the grace of our Baptism, is the norm for all genuine Christian praying.

Watch
with Me

an account of the prayer of Jesus in Gethsemane, he closely follows the version of Mark. At the same time he introduces many minor changes and some major ones. It is very enlightening to compare the two versions.

One of the main differences is the added emphasis on community and personal relationship that Matthew introduces. When he speaks of the disciples' coming loss of faith, he adds the words 'because of me' to emphasize that faith is a personal relationship with Jesus. They will not be able to cope with what happens to him in his Passion. Matthew is even free to tamper with the quote from the prophet Zechariah. 'The sheep will be scattered' becomes 'The sheep of the flock will be scattered' to stress the over-riding importance of community.

Central to Matthew's interest in community and relationship is his use of the tiny word 'with'. Its importance is underlined by its use in chapter one and again in the very last verse of the gospel: from 'He will be called God-with-us' (1:23) to 'I am with you always' (28:20). At the start of the Gethsemane account Matthew changes Mark's words 'they went' to 'Jesus went with them'. This use of 'with' takes on major importance when in Matthew's gospel it is added to the words of Jesus 'Could you not watch one hour?'

It is from the words in Matthew 'watch *with me* one hour', that the popular and mistaken exegesis arose that Jesus was finding his prayer too difficult, so he returned to the disciples looking for support. On the contrary, as in Mark, Jesus is filled with concern for the eleven, and interrupts his prayer to see if they are coping with their great time of trial and the temptation to lose faith in him. 'Watch and pray that you enter not into temptation.' It is through his deepening realization that they will give up and be scattered that Jesus is led to greater surrender to this hidden and most difficult will of his Father.

Mark tends to portray the humanness of Jesus more strikingly than the other three. He also tends to give more vivid details. Where Mark tell us that the initial state of Jesus on entering Gethsemane was one of 'terror', Matthew changes this to 'sadness'. Jesus, the Lord, can hardly be portrayed as being in such an extreme emotional state. He is much more in control. In Mark's gospel Jesus was stumbling on the ground; in Matthew's he prostrated in order to pray.

The greatest change which Matthew introduces to Mark's version is his spelling out more fully the words of the threefold prayer of Jesus. His prayer takes the form:

1) 'My Father, if it be possible, let this cup from me; nevertheless, not as I will, but as thou wilt.'

2) 'My Father, if this cannot pass until I drink it, thy will be done.'

3) 'Thy will be done.'

For the third time of prayer, Matthew remarks that Jesus prayed for the third time, saying the same words. This could be taken to mean all the words of the second prayer, but it seems far more likely that Matthew was trying to draw our attention to the last words of the second prayer. This would show the growth and development of the prayer of Jesus. In this interpretation, a real movement takes place in the inner attitude expressed in the three prayers above. In the first the word 'nevertheless' precedes the attachment to God's will. In the second there is a growing realization that the disciples will not persevere, so there is a short review of the situation (the cup cannot pass) before the expression of attachment to God's will. In the third there is the simple and profound resting in total surrender to that will.

In his account of Jesus at prayer Matthew provides us with the perfect model for our own prayer. Like Jesus, we must check out what is going on in us and around us as we pray. The will of God will be revealed to us, not so much by inner voices, but by insight into what is taking place in the real world. As we face the realities of our life situation, take these to God in prayer, and continue to struggle to say 'Thy will be done', there will be a change in us, so that we come to a deep peace in our union with God and are able to return to our life situation, however difficult it may be, in profound adherence to God's will.

This union and peace are far removed from a kind of grudging acceptance of God's will, because God is more powerful than we, and supposed to be wiser than we (though often we can't see it!). Like Jesus we are enabled to go forward peacefully in trust, even into death itself, which will always be the prelude to resurrection.

Prayer in
Agony

THE GOSPEL OF ST LUKE GIVES AN
account of the prayer of Jesus on the Mount of Olives, which is in
some ways like the versions of Mark and Matthew, and in other ways
very different.

The most obvious difference is the shorter form of Luke's version. We have seen previously that Luke gives more attention to prayer
in his gospel than the others do. So, here he can afford to be briefer.
There is no mention of Jesus praying three times, nor of the disciples'
repeatedly falling asleep.

A radical difference is that the disciples are much more faithful
in Luke's gospel than in the other three. At the time when Mark and
Matthew tell us about the disciples' coming loss of faith, and John
about their being scattered, Luke proclaims, 'You are the ones who
have continued with me in my trials; and I assign to you, as the Father
assigned to me, a kingdom, that you may eat and drink at my table in
my kingdom, and sit on thrones judging the twelve tribes of
Israel' (22:28-30).

In fact, in the gospel of Luke the eleven disciples do not run
away, but are present, with the women, at the crucifixion, watching it
all happen from a distance (23:49). Luke does mention that the

disciples slept while Jesus prayed, but he tries to excuse them by say-ing that they were 'sleeping for sorrow' (22:45).

As with Mark and Matthew, the central preoccupation of Jesus is that his apostles should pray to be preserved from the time of great trial and testing of their faith. In fact Luke has Jesus giving this in-struction to the disciples at both the beginning and the end of his own prayer. The passage in Luke has a very clear structure. Jesus in-structed the disciples to pray; he withdrew; he knelt; he prayed; he rose; he returned; he instructed the disciples to pray. The structure of the passage underlines the importance of the central act, the prayer of Jesus, and also the two 'bookends' of the framework: the need of the eleven to pray.

In Luke's account there are two very interesting verses (22:43-44), perhaps added by a later scribe, that are full of pictorial imagery and have really captured peoples' imagination. These are the verses about Jesus being in an agony, and therefore prolonging his prayer, his sweat becoming like drops of blood, and an angel coming to strengthen him. It is from Luke's use of the word 'agony' here that we get the usual name for the Gethsemane prayer, 'the agony in the garden'. Ironically 'garden' comes from the gospel of John, where there is no mention of Jesus's praying in that place, only the arrest in a garden.

Much has been written (mistakenly) about the 'sweat of blood'. Nowhere does the gospel say that Jesus sweated blood. But these verses say that Jesus broke into a perspiration that was *like* drops of blood, in being dark and heavy.

St Luke does not teach us about any change taking place in Jesus from a state of stress to one of peace and profound acceptance of the Father's will. The answer to his prayer is represented by the support he receives in his struggle from the 'angel from heaven'.

The word 'agony' and the sweat tell us about the great difficulty Jesus had in coming to terms with the events now overtaking him and his small community. The difficulty does not lead him to want to abandon his prayer. On the contrary, he prays more earnestly, at greater length. It is the common human experience in times of great stress that our prayer may not remove the obstacles and bring comfort, but there is nowhere else for us to be, nothing else that we can do, but stay praying in the void, the emptiness, the darkness.

Luke is well aware that while teaching about the effort that this cost Jesus, he must not give the impression that it was a sheer act of will power on his part. Hence the angel, strengthening him. Prayer is always answered. The angel represents the loving presence of the Father, keeping Jesus faithful to the reality of the present moment. I would suggest that this would be true at some times in the life of every praying person. There is no comfort anywhere, but there is the loving presence of our God, keeping us faithful. Disastrous events overwhelm us, so that we cannot sense or be aware of that presence, but the fact that our loving God is with us is revealed in the outcome: that in spite of pain and darkness, we persevere, not by our own strength, but in the strength given by God as answer to prayer.

There is another short text of scripture about the Gethsemane prayer, given in the Letter to the Hebrews 5:7-10. When the author writes of Jesus's praying 'aloud and in silent tears to the one who had the power to save him out of death', he chooses the tense of the Greek verb which shows that he is writing of one specific occasion on which Jesus prayed like this, namely in the Gethsemane prayer. Unlike most other translations which defer to our traditional, English phrase 'save him from death', the Jerusalem Bible correctly translates the Greek preposition 'save him *out of* death'.

The phrase 'out of death' is a clear reference to the resurrection. For the Hebrews, 'death' does not mean the act of dying, but Sheol, that mysterious realm of the dead. Our author goes on to say that because of the filial submission of Jesus his prayer was answered. *The* answer to the Gethsemane prayer is the resurrection. 'Being made perfect [by becoming the Lord], Jesus becomes the source of eternal life to all who obey *him*' (v. 9). Obedience is given now not only to 'the will of God', which an individual may rightly or wrongly claim to discern, but to the risen Lord, living in the community of the church.

The Answer
to Prayer

PRAYER IS ALWAYS ANSWERED. THE greatest example of prayer in the history of our world is the prayer of Jesus in Gethsemane. We ought to expect it to have the greatest answer.

As with Paul's earnest prayer to be freed from the 'sting of the flesh' (2 Corinthians ch.12), Jesus does not receive the direct answer he originally asked for. The hour and the cup do not pass. He dies. The disciples give up. The mission is not complete.

It might be instructive to look at several of the ways in which the prayer of Jesus is, in fact, answered.

1. His emotional state is changed from one of 'sudden terror and anguish' to one of peace and serenity.

2. He comes to a deeper union with God in the actual events of his life (the disciples' failure to watch).

3. He receives a revelation from the Father: that there is a deeper, though still hidden, meaning, in what is happening.

4. He is empowered to say with fuller meaning and deeper conviction, 'Thy will be done'. There has been a movement from adding

AT HOME WITH JESUS

'nevertheless thy will be done', as a qualification to the original prayer, to a state of profound adherence to the will of God in what is taking place.

5. 'He learned to obey in the school of suffering' (Hebrews 5:8). The word obey literally means 'really to hear'. 'He learned to obey' does not, of course, imply that he was ever disobedient. It does underline the important truth that Jesus, like us, must take time and painstaking prayer to hear what the Father is saying in the new events that have overtaken him. He cannot simply hand the Father a blank cheque ahead of time. He must learn through suffering, that is, through human experience, and in spending time and effort working through the experience.

6. When Jesus does hear what the Father is saying, the answer is clearly 'Trust me; leave it in my hands'.

7. The Resurrection. He prayed to 'the one who had the power to save him out of death. He submitted so humbly that his prayer was heard' (Hebrews 5:7). Unlike other translations which say 'save him from death', the Jerusalem Bible correctly translates the Greek preposition: 'out of death'—that is, out of the realm of the dead. This is a clear reference to the Resurrection.

8. The mission, in fact, does not fail. The disciples do reunite. The Spirit is sent. The Kingdom is coming, and will certainly come definitively.

Some of the implications for our own prayer life are obvious. Like Jesus we must bring to our prayer the truly significant events of our world—both global and personal. Like him we ought to be concerned not so much about ourselves, even in the face of death, as for the coming of the Kingdom. All genuine Christian prayer is prayer for others. I pray for myself in order to be a better instrument on mission for the coming of the Kingdom.

It is necessary, through reflection, to be aware of what is happening in order to bring it to God in prayer. This is the process that Ignatius follows throughout his Spiritual Exercises. Reflect. Pray. Reflect. And the cycle is repeated indefinitely. In this

88

way the real Kingdom of God comes in our real world.

We pray spontaneously for what we think we need. If we are open to God and to the course of events, we become aware that our prayer needs to be modified, to grow and develop. It becomes more clear to us what God's will in fact is. So, we are able to pray 'Thy will be done', not in some vague, general kind of way, but in the challenge to accept that will as it becomes concretely clearer in the events of life.

There is always the challenge to our faith really to believe that our prayer is answered. Is there really Someone on the other end of this telephone? We have just seen that, although Jesus must still go to his death and the disciples will still run away, his prayer receives at least eight answers. Some of these answers are infallibly linked to all prayer. Every time I pray, I am changed. I receive revelation from God. I learn to obey. God always answers, 'Trust me'. I grow in union with God. I receive the power of the Lord's Spirit.

All praying people are aware that God's action is not so much to perform miracles 'out there' for us, but to change our inner attitudes, so that we are more ready to accept serenely what cannot be changed, and to notice the previously hidden ways that God is acting in our world.

Pray in
My Name

'THE FATHER WILL GRANT YOU anything you ask him in my name' (John 15:16). These words of Jesus occur three times in John's gospel: in chapters 14, 15 and 16. What a consolation for people of prayer. All I have to do is to pray in the name of Jesus and what I want will be granted. This statement is certainly true, but the words, as usual in John's gospel, have a very deep meaning. Let us explore that meaning.

John would agree wholeheartedly if I were to say, 'Every time that I pray I receive a revelation from God'. Revelation is *the* theme of John's gospel. 'No-one has ever seen God; the only Son who is closest to the Father's heart has made him known' (John 1:18). Jesus comes from the Father into the world, and his mission is to reveal who he himself is. In doing this he reveals who the Father is. The word 'reveal' here does not mean simply to give us information, but to communicate to us divine life. The constantly recurring phrase that John uses to describe this kind of life is 'eternal life'.

In the first chapter of John's gospel we have the story of two young men who go out to listen to the preaching of John the Baptist. Like typical tertiary student types, on the verge of their lives, they are looking for people who can stimulate them in their search for the meaning of life. So they go to hear the popular preacher of the day. He points out to them a greater teacher, Jesus; so they follow him. When he catches them following him and asks what they want. They reply, 'Where do you live?' This is John's way of saying that, without really knowing it, they were seeking and asking Jesus for eternal life.

Everyone in John's gospel wants eternal life: the Samaritan woman (chapter 4), Nicodemus (chapter 5), the Jews (chapter 6), even Pilate. If he had waited for an answer to his question, 'What is truth?', perhaps he would have heard Jesus reply, 'I am the way, the truth and the life'. What is this eternal life that everyone wants? John gives the answer in chapter 17: 'This is eternal life, to know you, the only true God, and Jesus Christ, whom you have sent' (17:3). The word 'eternal' here does not refer just to life that goes on and on, beyond the grave, but to a *quality* of life that we have already, now, in this world.

'Anything you ask in my name ...' Drawing its theology from texts like this, and the words of Paul in Colossians 3:17, 'Whatever you do, in word or deed, do everything in the name of the Lord Jesus, giving thanks to God the Father through him', the church in its liturgy concludes all its prayer to the Father with the formula 'through Jesus Christ, our Lord'. But the statement of John has a far deeper and richer meaning than simply adding these words to every prayer that we make.

In ancient Jewish culture the name represented the power or impact of the person. In both the gospel and the letters John never tires of repeating that the Lord Jesus dwells in the Christian. He and I are one. So, to pray in his name means to make a prayer in touch with that union, a prayer that is conscious of and arises out of that union. Such prayer is infallible. It must be answered. My union with the Lord, my knowledge of him, my hold on eternal life will infallibly be deepened.

But I prayed to win the lottery, or, more seriously, that my friend with cancer would recover. Will that prayer be granted? Every time I pray I grow in union with Jesus, and in a loving knowledge of what he wants for me. No matter what I ask, I come to a deeper union with him with regard to that very thing. As we well know, this may or may not involve my friend's recovery, or the winning of the lottery. But it does involve more eternal life. And that is really what I am praying for; that is what every praying person really wants.

It is true to say that the fruit of my prayer is greater union with Jesus, not in a vague, general sort of way, but in the very mundane matter that I prayed about. The Jesus with whom I have grown in intimacy is interested in everything that I am interested in. We meet heart to heart on truly common ground.

The Hour
Has Come

IT IS TYPICAL OF THE GOSPEL OF JOHN
that the author takes the traditions and stories about Jesus common
to the other gospels and uses them in a new, free and creative way.
This is precisely what he does with the great prayer of Jesus before his
suffering and death. He divides his treatment of it into two parts, one
in chapter twelve, one in chapter seventeen. The first is set in the
Temple and the second at the table of the Last Supper. But, as we shall
see, they are one and the same prayer as the Gethsemane of the synoptic gospels.

In the twelfth chapter of John some Greeks approach Philip with
the simple request that they wish to see Jesus. The word 'see' is a very
important one for John. It means to believe in Jesus. When he hears
their request, Jesus is reminded that it is only through his death and
resurrection that such believing is possible. So, the request of these
Greek visitors to Jerusalem leads Jesus to face up to his coming death
and all that that implies. In this section of the twelfth chapter John
very creatively puts together three key elements from the synoptic
gospels of Jesus's preparation for his Passion: the sayings about discipleship, the Transfiguration (the voice from heaven of verse 28) and
the struggle of the Gethsemane prayer.

A key word for the gospel of John is the word 'hour'.

The whole gospel tells the story of the entry of the Word made flesh into our world and then, at the *hour*, his passing out of the world to the Father. So, Jesus speaks of his coming death (12:23) as the hour when he is to be glorified. Very rightly it is not the dying, but the coming glorification that is the focus of his attention.

Jesus then gives us everybody's favourite parable—just a one-liner—'Unless a grain of wheat falls into the ground and dies, it remains a single grain; but, if it dies, it yields a rich harvest' (12:24). Joined to this is the only saying of Jesus that appears in all four gospels: 'Anyone who loves their life will lose it; anyone who hates their life in this world will keep it for eternal life'. Clearly the word 'hate' here refers to true spiritual freedom and detachment.

As in the synoptic stories of Gethsemane, Jesus now proclaims, as a prelude to his prayer, that his soul is troubled. As in John's immediately preceding story of the raising of Lazarus, it is not so much the fact of death and dying that causes Jesus to be troubled and to weep, as the symbolism involved in death. Death involves for all of us a confrontation with ultimate reality and with the effects of evil. Jesus is now involved in the ultimate struggle against the forces of evil to bring the very delicate gift of faith for those who are seeking it. This means he must go to his death; he must leave his disciples; in his death evil will appear to triumph and his mission to fail. John will shortly report that Jesus left the people and went into hiding (12:36). 'Though they had been present when he did so many signs, they did not believe into him' (12:37). This failure of his followers to come to committed faith, as in the synoptics, is the real cause of the distress of Jesus; it is much more than the simple human fear of dying.

What prayer does Jesus offer in the face of this horrendous struggle with evil? He himself asks the question, 'What shall I say?' As always, he turns to the Father, and prays, 'Father, save me out of this hour'. He is to enter into his hour in union with a loving Father who will bring salvation, resurrection for him out of the hour.

The prayer of Jesus here is not to be saved *from* the hour. There is a saving for him not only beyond the hour, but even *in* the hour. His prayer is equivalent to saying: 'Keep me safe right through this hour'. Throughout our most dreadful human experiences, in all of the suffering, even in the moment of dying, we are in the Father's loving, saving care. For John the passion and dying of Jesus are not a moment of defeat, but one of triumph. Each of us, in our prayer, can go to this hidden depth, where we no longer simply hope for salvation *after* disaster, but know that what 'the world' regards as disaster is indeed the saving act of God.

This consciousness of the saving, loving presence of the Father brings Jesus through his trouble back to his starting-point: focus on the coming glorification. He concludes his prayer with the words, 'Father, glorify your name'. As we saw with Mark, Matthew and Luke, the Gethsemane prayer is a repetition of the Lord's Prayer. Here it is again: Father, glorify thy name—the equivalent of 'hallowed be thy name'.

As we shall see, in chapter seventeen the time of trouble and struggle for Jesus is over (that has been dealt with in chapter twelve). He is able to start with 'Father, glorify your name' and go on to spell out the depth and richness contained in those wonderful words. The simplicity of the Lord's Prayer will be revealed to contain the greatest depths of Christian mysticism.

The Lord's
Prayer in
St John

AS A CHRISTIAN, MY PRAYER IS NOT
primarily *my* activity; rather it is the activity of God at work in me.
Under the title of Father, God is seen as the one whose love initiates
everything in creation.

This is especially true of that activity which we call prayer. The
Father is active, inviting me, prompting me to turn to him in prayer.
When I do pray, the Holy Spirit, who lives in me through my Bap-
tism, is praying in me.

This is the great teaching of Romans chapter eight. It is the Spirit
of the risen Lord Jesus in the heart of the Christian who cries out to
God, 'Abba! Father!' (Romans 8:15-16; Galatians 4:6). When we don't
know how to pray, the same Spirit 'intercedes for us with sighs too
deep for words' (Romans 8:26). So the Christian is one with Jesus at
prayer. Jesus and I pray together. This is why we so value *his* prayer,
the Lord's Prayer. It is not because we have an accurate record of the
words the Lord spoke—we don't! It is because this prayer situates us
where we truly belong: within the life of the Blessed Trinity itself.

We pray with Jesus. John, in the seventeenth chapter of his gos-

96

pel, gives us one prayer of Jesus at great length and in detail. It is so profound that it is not easy to understand, but what a treasure it is, and how well worth the effort of examining it carefully.

John frequently treats the stories of the life of Jesus with a freedom and a creativity that goes beyond that of the other three gospel writers. He does not give us the Lord's Prayer in the form of the Our Father (Matthew) or the simple, direct form of Luke, but this chapter seventeen is clearly the same prayer more fully and profoundly spelt out.

This prayer is also clearly the same as the Gethsemane prayer of the other three gospel writers. John has divided that prayer of Jesus into two parts. We have already considered the first part from the twelfth chapter of the gospel, in which John treats of the sorrow and struggle of Jesus. Now, in chapter seventeen, that has been worked through, and the focus is on the final stage of the Gethsemane prayer, 'Thy will be done', in order to spell out the profound meaning of that phrase.

The timing of the prayer is the same for John as for the others: immediately before the arrest, which takes place in a garden. John is the only one who uses that word which has become traditional in the phrase 'agony in the garden'. The context is the same: Jesus is reflecting on the fact that his supremely self-confident disciples will soon be scattered. 'The time is coming, indeed it has come, when you will be scattered, each one going his own way and leaving me alone' (John 16:32). As a result, the prayer of Jesus will focus especially on his concern that the disciples should not lose faith and separate, the same concern that is shown in the synoptics when he kept trying to keep them awake and on the watch.

The setting of the prayer is different: for John, at the table of the Last Supper; for the others, after leaving the supper and going across the valley to the slope of the Mount of Olives.

We see that the prayer of Jesus in John 17 is the same as the Gethsemane prayer. We have already seen the latter is simply an expression of the Lord's Prayer. In the case of John 17 the identification with the Lord's Prayer is strikingly clear. The Our Father has three parts: the address to the Father, the three petitions that the Father accomplish his purpose in us (or hallow his name), the petitions for our great needs (deliverance from evil). In John 17 the address 'Father' is repeated no fewer than six times; the two dominant themes of the prayer are the petition to the Father to glorify (hallow) his name, and to preserve the disciples in the face of temptation and evil. In fact we have in verse 15 the final words of the Our Father: 'deliver them from evil'.

Just as we treasure the Our Father, this great prayer of the gospel of John should be precious to all Christians. It is the Lord's Prayer in another form. Because of its length it is able to spell out the richness and depth of that prayer. In fact, it is John's or Jesus's own commentary on the Our Father.

St John's gospel commences the account of the Last Supper (13:1) by announcing that 'the hour has come for Jesus to pass out of this world to the Father'. This becomes the setting for our Eucharistic Prayer IV: 'When the time came for him to be glorified by you, his heavenly Father ...' So Jesus commences the great prayer of John 17 with the words, 'Father, the hour has come'. We, too, can commence every prayer with the same words. *Now* is always God's hour for us.

Every hour is or can be a moment of suffering and of glorification with our Lord. These realities are never far away from the living of our 'ordinary' lives. 'Hour' is a rich, symbolic word in all four gospels. For Mark and Matthew, it is the hour for Jesus to be handed over into the hands of sinners. For Luke, it is the hour of the seeming triumph of Satan and 'the powers of darkness'. For John, it is the hour of glorification.

One of the most significant lines in the gospel of John is this saying of Jesus: 'When the Son of Man has been lifted up from the earth, then you will know that I am He' (8:28). It is precisely this 'lifting up' from the earth that will fulfil the mission of Jesus—to reveal who he is, and so who the Father is. For John 'lifting up' clearly has a double meaning. Jesus is to be lifted up on the cross, and at the same time to be lifted up into glory. For John the crucifixion *is* the glorification. It is on the cross that Jesus gives the Spirit . 'He handed over the spirit' (19:30) is another of John's famous, powerful 'double meanings'.

Jesus asks the Father to glorify him (17:1), not for his own sake, but in order that he may glorify the Father. He is, in effect, asking the Father to glorify his own name. This is the dominant theme of John 17—the same as 'Hallowed be thy name' in the Lord's Prayer of Luke and Matthew. We saw, when reflecting on the Lord's Prayer, that the three phrases, 'Hallowed be thy name', 'Thy kingdom come' and 'Thy will be done', really mean one and the same thing. Here, in verse 2, John clearly spells out that meaning: 'Through the power over all humankind that you have given to him, let him give eternal life to all those you have entrusted to him'. The Father hallows his name, brings about his kingdom and accomplishes his will by sharing with us, his people, his own life.

The Father accomplishes this eternal purpose of his through Christ, his Son, whom he has sent on mission. Jesus then passes that mission on to his disciples and through them to us. For John, 'those you have entrusted to him' (v.9) means primarily the group of disciples, Jesus's own community. Most of this great prayer will focus on them. But Jesus also includes 'those who through their word will believe in me' (v. 20). Each of us, therefore, shares in the mission to give eternal life to those who are entrusted to us: the members of our own families, all those with whom we are in relationship, and, through the power of our prayer, the whole world. As I pray with Jesus, my prayer, too, must be not for myself, but for the coming of the kingdom, for my particular share in communicating the gift of eternal life to all to whom I am sent, just as Jesus was sent.

The third verse of the prayer gives us Jesus's definition of eternal life: 'to know you, the only true God, and Jesus Christ whom you have sent'. The knowledge of the Father and of the Son is, of course, the one knowledge, implanted in the heart of the praying person by the gift of the Holy Spirit. 'If you know me, you know my Father too … To have seen me is to have seen the Father' (14:7-9). The knowledge referred to is 'heart knowledge'. The main characteristic of such knowledge is *love*. The Holy Spirit, who is life and is the bond of love beween Father and Son, comes to us with that gift of knowledge that is part of that classic list of gifts of the Holy Spirit we receive in our Confirmation.

Already, in only three verses, the seventeenth chapter of John has give us material for reflection and prayer that leads us deeply into our sharing in the life of the Trinity itself. In the fourth verse Jesus proclaims that he has glorified the Father (hallowed his name) on earth, and finished the work, completed the mission, given to him by the Father. Throughout this prayer there is a free movement back and forth from the time before the passion to the time after the resurrection. It is in his glory, now, that Jesus has completed the mission. Jesus tells the Father that it time for the Father to give him the glory Jesus had with the Father from all eternity. This refers, not to his glory as eternal Son (he'd never lost that), but to the glorification of his humanity that the Father had willed for him from the very beginning.

For John the mission of Jesus is to reveal who the Father is, to make his name known, to glorify (or hallow) his name. Jesus does this by revealing who he himself is. Just as the Lord God of the Old Testament had revealed himself as 'I am', so in John's gospel Jesus proclaims over and over again: 'I am'… the bread of life, the light of the world, the good shepherd, the gate of the sheepfold, the resurrection and the life, the vine, the way, the truth and the life. Walking on the water, Jesus reassures his disciples with the words, 'Fear not; I am'. He even declares, 'Before Abraham was, I am'. And, very importantly, 'When the Son of Man has been lifted up from the earth, then you will know that I am' (8:28).

So, Jesus has certainly made the Father's name known, but there is far more to that revelation than simply repeating the words 'I am', words which had been used in the book of Exodus to show that God is, in fact, beyond all naming. Jesus has made the Father's name known by sharing the Father's life with his disciples. This sharing of life becomes the main theme of the final part of this prayer.

Jesus now begins to express in his prayer his concern for his disciples. Very beautifully he tells the Father: 'They were yours and you gave them to me' (v. 6). At the end of chapter sixteen, in pre-Passion mode, he was telling them that they were all going to be scattered. Now, in post-Resurrection mode, he is proclaiming, 'They have kept your word … at last they know … they have believed'. They belong to the Father, and it is in them that Jesus is glorified. This post-

Resurrection era continues to the present day, and it is in us, his Body, that Jesus is now glorified.

In pre-Passion mode, as in the Gethsemane prayer of Mark, Matthew and Luke, Jesus now focuses on the neediness of his disciples, their weakness and the fragility of their faith. Here John uses the word 'world' to signify the evil which threatens to snuff out the faith of the disciples. This is a different, symbolic use of this word from that in John 3:16, the text so dear to the heart of the Christian evangelizer who holds those famous numbers aloft on a banner at every Olympic Games: 'God so loved the world that he gave his only begotten Son, so that whoever believes into him may not perish, but have eternal life'.

Verses 11 and 12 introduce the great theme of communion: 'Holy Father, keep those you have given me in your name, that they may be one, even as we are one. While I was with them, I kept them in your name, which you have given to me'. All of this throws light on the words 'Hallowed be thy name' of the Lord's Prayer. The Father hallows his name by sharing his own life with the followers of Jesus. The word 'name' means the life of the person. Life was given to Jesus by the Father, and he passed it on to the disciples. It is still being passed on today. With all this in mind Jesus prays first for his disciples and then for all his future disciples.

Jesus prays that the Father will keep those he has entrusted to him true to his name—equivalent to asking the Father to continue to share his life with them, that is, to hallow his name in them. He goes on to ask that they be protected from evil, or the evil one (v. 15), so that the parallel with the Lord's Prayer of Matthew is complete.

The chapter concludes with a lengthy prayer for 'all those who through their word will believe in me' (vv. 20-26). Their 'word' (singular) is the carrying out of their mission, the quality of their witness, rather than their spoken words. The Father is in Jesus, Jesus in the Father, both of them in us and we live in both of them. John keeps repeating the various combinations of this indwelling to invite us, his readers, to go deeply into the contemplation of this reality and to make the prayer of Jesus our own.

Lectio Divina

THE LATIN NAME *LECTIO DIVINA* comes from the rule of St Benedict. A literal English translation is 'divine reading'. Reading, however is only the beginning. The aim of the lectio in the Benedictine tradition is to become thoroughly steeped in sacred truth, so as to live one's life by that truth. There is much more involved here than a 'method of prayer'; *lectio divina* is a way of life.

The material for the *lectio* was almost always sacred Scripture, sometimes the Fathers of the Church, and more rarely other spiritual writings. The effect was often seen as a fulfilment of the words of Psalm 37:30: 'The mouth of the virtuous will murmur wisdom'.

As Peter the Venerable wrote of the holy brother Benedict: 'Without rest his lips ruminated the sacred words'. And the abbot John writing about Blessed John of Gorze: 'With hushed murmuring after the fashion of the buzz of the bee, he would continuously repeat the psalms'. The *lectio* is to fill the mind and the heart, so that response to God flows readily and constantly, transforming our way of speaking and acting.

The steps involved in this form of prayer are variously described by different authors, ranging from three: reading, meditation, prayer, to six: reading, thought, study, meditation, prayer, contemplation. It should be clear that there is a gradual depthing involved on the way from reading to contemplation. Reading is not an end in itself. In the shorter analysis of the *lectio* reading will always involve thought and study (*cogitatio* and *studium*) leading into meditation. The thinking and the study involved here are not of a purely abstract or academic kind, but are geared to the ever deepening movement towards God.

A classic treatment of the subject is given by the ninth Carthusian prior of Grande Chartreuse, Guigo II, who died in 1188. Guigo wrote to another monk 'A Letter on the Interior Life', which is sometimes given the name 'The Ladder of Monks'. Guigo sees it as analogous to Jacob's ladder (Genesis 28:12). 'Its lower end rests upon the earth, but its top pierces the clouds and touches heavenly secrets.' This ladder has four rungs: reading, meditation, prayer and contemplation. Like the great St Bernard (died 1153) and his followers, for whom the interior sense of taste dominated one's use of Scripture, Guigo draws on the imagery of eating to describe the four stages. 'Reading, as it were, presents solid food; Meditation chews it; Prayer acquires the flavour; Contemplation is the sweetness itself.'

Elsewhere he writes: 'Seek by reading and you will find by meditating; knock by praying and it will be opened to you in contemplating'. 'Reading is the careful study of the scriptures, concentrating all one's powers on it. Meditation is the busy application of the mind to seek with the help of one's reason for knowledge of hidden truth. Prayer is the heart's devoted turning to God to do away with evil and obtain what is good. Contemplation occurs when the mind is in some sort lifted up to God and held above itself, so that it tastes the joys of everlasting sweetness.'

Reading and meditation alert the praying person to the possibilty of experiencing the joy and sweetness that the Word of God contains and promises, but at the same time one is aware of being unable to attain what one longs for. Longing and desire are acutely felt, but one is at an impasse, so that the only possibility is to turn to the Lord in prayer, the third rung, and earnestly beg for what is desired. What is the Lord's answer to such prayer?

'The Lord, whose eyes are upon the just, and whose ears catch not only their words (Psalm 34:15; 1 Peter 3:12), but the very meaning of their prayers, does not wait until the longing soul has said all its say, but breaks in upon the middle of its prayer, runs to meet it in haste, sprinkled with the heavenly dew, anointed with the most precious perfumes; and he restores the weary soul, he slakes its thirst, he feeds its hunger, he makes the soul forget all earthly things: by making it die to itself he gives it new life in a wonderful way, and by making it drunk he brings it to its true senses.' This is Guigo's description of the effects of what he calls 'this exalted contemplation'.

Lest we think that all is now 'sweetness and light', there are two things to point out about the consolation experienced here: first, it may take the painful form of tears, effecting a cleansing of our inner selves; second, it is not an end it itself. Guigo is careful to point out that the Lord who reveals himself in this way will soon withdraw and leave us to struggle after purity of conscience without the experience of sweetness.

'Let a person beware lest after contemplation, in which one has been lifted to the very heavens, one plunge violently into the depths, and after such graces turn again to the sinful pleasures of the world and the delights of the flesh. Since however the soul has not the power to bear for long the shining of the true light, let it descend gently and in due order to one or other of the three degrees by means of which it made its ascent: let it rest now in one, now in another, as the circumstances of time and place suggest to its free choice.'

Since the 1960s when modern translations of Scripture became available for the first time, many millions of Christians have followed the practice of prayerful reading of the text of Scripture, pausing and delighting wherever they have found nourishment. This form of prayer, following the beginning steps of the *lectio*, was strongly recommended in the Dogmatic Constitution on Divine Revelation of Vatican II:

'All clerics, particularly priests of Christ and others who, as deacons or catechists, are officially engaged in the ministry of the Word, should immerse themselves in the Scriptures by constant sacred reading and diligent study. For it must not happen that anybody becomes "an empty preacher of the Word of God to others, not being a hearer of the Word in his own heart" (St Augustine), when he ought to be sharing the boundless riches of the divine Word with the faithful committed to his care, especially in the sacred liturgy. Likewise, the sacred synod forcefully and specifically exhorts all the Christian faithful, especially those who live the religious life, to learn "the surpassing knowledge of Jesus Christ" (Philippians 3:8) by frequent reading of the divine Scriptures. "Ignorance of the Scriptures is ignorance of Christ" (St Jerome). Therefore let them go gladly to the sacred text itself, whether in the sacred liturgy, which is full of the divine words, or in devout reading, or in such suitable exercises and various other helps which, with the approval and guidance of the pastors of the church, are happily spreading everywhere in our day. Let them remember, however, that prayer should accompany the reading of sacred Scripture, so that a dialogue takes place between God and the person. "For we speak to God when we pray; we listen to God when we read the divine oracles" (St Ambrose)' (*Verbum Dei*, 25).

This instruction has been amply put into practice and has borne abundant fruit. However, there remains the temptation to linger over the poetry and felicitous wording of a passage of Scripture. We are always called to go further. As Guigo puts it, referring to the four rungs of the ladder, 'the first degrees are of little or no use without the last, while the last can never or hardly ever be won without the first'.

Praying with
The Cloud

contemplative prayer life of Christians is the small book, *The Cloud of Unknowing*, by an anonymous English author of the fourteenth century. With the rediscovery of contemplation by many 'ordinary' people in recent years, the importance and relevance of this little book is greater than ever.

Like anyone encouraging contemplation, the author writes for people who are striving for purity of conscience and are committed to a life of prayer and union with God. No techniques are of any use for anyone who would like to dabble in contemplation or have some sort of new and interesting experience.

The Cloud of Unknowing is in the tradition of what is called the negative way in theology, the way of the book 'Mystical Theology' of pseudo-Dionysius, the unknown writer, perhaps from Syria in the sixth century, whose writing has influenced not only the author of *The Cloud*, but the great Carmelite tradition of the sixteenth century. God is infinitely beyond all human images and concepts. So, whenever we make a positive affirmation about God (God is good, for instance), we must immediately add, 'God's goodness is not like any created goodness'. Unlike the agnostics we can make valid statements about God, but what we cannot grasp far exceeds what we can know about God.

This is true about theology (it was declared by the Second Lateran Council in 1215); it is even more true about our experiential knowledge of God in contemplation. We do not set out on the journey of prayer to gain knowledge about God or about ourselves, but to deepen a relationship of love. In another work, *The Book of Privy Counselling*, the author of *The Cloud* declares that I must not seek to know who I am or who is God when engaged in this work: 'Think of God as you do of yourself, and of yourself as you do of God: that God is as God is, and you are as you are, so that your thought is not separated or scattered, but oned in the One that is all'.

Between God and the person contemplating is a cloud of unknowing. There is no human way of penetrating this cloud. So, if in prayer a thought or image of God comes to mind, I must banish it to a cloud beneath me, called the cloud of forgetting. It is a good thing to have good and holy thoughts and images, but not when I am engaged in being in union with God through contemplation. Of course, all distractions and other thoughts and images must also be dismissed into the cloud of forgetting.

The contemplative person must remain between the cloud of unknowing above and the cloud of forgetting beneath, staying in what is classically known as the mystical silence. Is there anything we can do in this situation? Yes, says our author. The key is desire. We must let our longing beat upon the cloud of unknowing, and so pierce the cloud with the 'keen shaft of love'. Love is the essence of the whole enterprise, what the author calls 'a naked intent towards God for his own sake'. It is 'naked' because, even though our desire is enflamed with love, it is not clothed in any thought. We experience the 'blind stirring of love'; once again, it is blind because it does not proceed by the way of knowing, but the way of unknowing.

It is presumed that our praying person has gone through the ordinary stages of use of scripture, spiritual reading and reflection, leading to prayer. The more one advances in contemplation, the simpler the prayer will become. A contemplative will then pray with just one word, as in the 'mantra' style of prayer, recently popularized by

Benedictine, John Main. Unlike Main our author strongly recommends the use of a monosyllable, like 'Sin', 'Help', 'God'. Here again, he is not talking about technique, but this short, simple prayer is efficacious because it involves the pray-er's whole desire and being, like the drowning person's cry of 'Help!'

While the author of *The Cloud* gives us a way of contemplative prayer, he is always careful to insist that God deals with different persons differently, and the gift of contemplation is always precisely that, a free gift from God, not for all, but often given to those who truly desire it. Anyone who is advancing in prayer would profit from reading *The Cloud*, not in order to find a new technique, but to enrich their own personal gift.

The author concludes his book by asking how a person would know if they are called to pray in this way. As always, the key is desire. If you read the book and really want to pray in this way, then pray in this way. Even for praying people who have not set out deliberately to follow the way of *The Cloud*, there will be times in their life of contemplation when the experience will be not one of thought, image or feeling, but of the utter hiddenness of God. When we find ourselves in this situation, our author is a sure guide on the way forward to union with God.

All Will
Be Well

IF WE ARE LOOKING TO JOIN IN PRAYER
with someone who is outstanding for graciousness, joy and gentleness, we should look no further than the great English hermit and contemplative of the fourteenth century, Blessed Julian of Norwich. Her optimism, founded in authentic Christian hope, seems particularly suited to the needs of our present age. Of all her sayings, the most often repeated is her contant refrain, 'All will be well; all will be well; all manner of thing will be well'. Her other constantly repeated theme is, 'God keeps us most surely'.

At the age of thirty, desiring to share in our Lord's sufferings, Julian took the radical and somewhat unusual step of praying for a serious illness. God duly obliged, and for three days she lay at death's door. At this time she received from God sixteen revelations, which she describes in her classic work, *The Revelations of Divine Love*.

The principal vision or image that came to Julian at this time was of our Lord in his Passion. For Julian, suffering is linked with joy, and she sees Jesus smiling through his suffering and through the blood he sheds (she is always careful to describe accurately what she sees). No matter what Julian writes about, whether it is sin or suffering or desolation in prayer—and she is utterly realistic—

it is always from the perspective of hope, trust, joy and fulfilment.

The revelations provide us with a profound teaching in spiritual theology. Part of the first revelation and all of the fourteenth are on the subject of prayer. In the first Julian sees that it is far more pleasing to God (her words are 'delightful to him'!) that we should cleave to God's goodness with steadfast faith rather than use all the methods that people can devise. Authentic prayer is not a matter of method, but of clinging in faith to God's goodness. Devotion to the Passion and to Mary, both of which are most precious to Julian, are only worthwhile because they are gifts that come to us from God's goodness.

This is always the essential element of prayer: the goodness of God.

All the help that we receive from devotion to the saints comes from the goodness of God. It is indeed pleasing to God that we seek God by all the ordinary means of devotion, but understanding all the time that God is the goodness of them all. 'The highest prayer is to the goodness of God that comes down to us, to the lowest part of our need.'

The fourteenth revelation begins with the divine initiative, something that for Julian is always exquisite, courteous and gracious. Indeed the quality of her spirituality is conveyed through her command of the elegant English prose of her day. The Lord declares to her: 'I am the ground of your prayer. I make you desire it; I make you ask for it, and you do ask for it. How could it be then you do not obtain what you ask for?' Julian is very clear about this infallibility of prayer. 'Nothing is more impossible than that we should seek mercy and grace and not have it.'

Because of this certainty of having our prayer answered, Julian insists on perseverance in prayer, even when we lack all feeling for it. The Lord speaks to her: 'Pray inwardly, though there seem to be no relish in it. Though you should feel naught, pray inwardly. Though you see naught, though it seems you cannot pray because of dryness and barrenness, pray inwardly. In sickness and weakness your prayer is fully pleasing to me, though you have little savour for it, and so all your living is a prayer in my sight.'

Closely linked to God's initiative, to the certainty of prayer's answer and to perseverance, is thanksgiving. 'Thanksgiving is a true inward knowing, a turning of ourselves with great reverence and with all our power to the working our Lord stirs in us, giving thanks inwardly with joy.'

For Julian there are three important lessons to learn about prayer. The first is that our prayer is God's doing. God takes the initiative. 'I am the ground of it; it is my will.' Secondly, there is our part in it, which is to unite our will with God's will in joy. Notice that it is not a matter of submitting grudgingly, but always with joy. Thirdly, the fruit of our prayer is that we will be 'oned'—made one—and like to our Lord in everything. As always with Julian, there is total certainty about her trust in this outcome. 'It is our Lord's will that our trust and our prayer be alike, large. To be lacking in trust is to fail in true worship of our Lord in prayer; and also we hinder and hurt ourselves.'

Julian is very clear about God's gifting of us, God's present activity in our lives and the certainty of our salvation. 'As we behold all that God has done with thanksgiving, we ought to pray for the deed that he is now a-doing: that is that he rule and guide us in this life, to his worship, and bring us to his bliss.' The goal of our prayer is to make our will one with God's in joy, and, when this happens, 'all our intent and all our might is set wholly on the beholding of him'.

Of Weal and Woe

MOST OF US LEARNED TO PRAY 'at our mother's knee'. What usually happened at that knee was that we were taught to make the Sign of the Cross, and to say the 'Our Father' and 'Hail Mary'. Of course, there was far more to mother's lesson than that. We learned to be reverent like her, we learned that prayer was important and special, that God and Jesus are real persons to whom we can speak. However, the main feature for most people is that they were launched on a lifetime programme of 'saying their prayers'.

Once we move beyond 'saying prayers' and enter upon meditation or contemplation, listening or a prayer of quiet, we begin to notice how we feel in our relationship with God. God is no longer just someone to talk to. We must listen, be aware of our feelings, and take the kind of risks that are involved in any personal relationship. My prayer life is now moving more out of my control. I must be open to whatever kind of experience my time of prayer may bring. That means being open to a whole range of ordinary, and sometimes extraordinary, thoughts and feelings.

St Ignatius, the master of discernment of spirits, draws our attention to the two main kinds of movement we experience in prayer, which he calls consolation and desolation. Consolation is an inner movement of my thoughts or feelings, or still deeper, my spirit, which is moving me towards God. It is often accompanied by a felt peace and joy, so that spirituality seems easy and delightful. Desolation is exactly the opposite. My thoughts, feelings and my spirit are moving away from God. It is often accompanied by darkness and confusion, so that spirituality seems like an impossible burden.

In the fourteenth century, Julian of Norwich wrote with great clarity and power in her seventh revelation of what she calls 'weal' (consolation) and 'woe' (desolation). Like all praying people Julian experienced each of these very many times. Her descriptions of them accurately fit the praying experience of people today. The 'weal' 'was so glad and spiritual a feeling that I was all in peace, in ease and in rest, so that there was nothing in earth that might have grieved me'. In time of 'woe' 'I was left to myself, feeling the heaviness and weariness of life, and irksomeness of myself, so that I scarcely had patience to live'. She notices also that the cycles of consolation and desolation come in quick succession, and unexpectedly, without any warning. In the good times nothing seems too difficult; she is filled with confidence. She thinks that 'no pain that I might possibly experience could have dis-eased me'.

Trust in God, faith, gratitude, confidence, the fruit of the Spirit, all these realities 'come alive' for us. We know that we are in touch with reality, with the truth. The truths of faith, the work of the Holy Spirit, our feelings and our spirit are all moving harmoniously in the same direction. This 'makes sense'. It *seems* only reasonable that this happy state should continue without interruption.

Then, surprisingly, consolation disappears, and we are subject to doubt, darkness, confusion, negative feelings, anger, guilt, fear. The list seems endless. Not only that; the desolation has a dynamism about it. Most often it starts out as a tiny doubt: 'Am I really praying, or am I just imagining it all, just talking to myself?' As I begin to listen to this small voice of doubt, I begin to enter into a downward spiral, so that not only is there no way out, but there is a pull, moving ever more quickly in the direction of depression and despair. How am I to cope?

Julian advises us to reflect and to be convinced ahead of the time of woe that 'God keepeth us surely, ever the same, in woe and in weal', and that it is necessary and profitable that we have both kinds of experience. The God who gives the feelings of consolation is the same God who allows us to experience the desolation. 'Both are the one love.'

It is God's will that we remain in consolation as much as we possibly can. This is the normal state of someone who is trying to be a true disciple of the Lord. 'For bliss lasts without end; whilst pain is passing, and shall be brought to naught in those that shall be saved. Therefore it is not God's will that we keep step with our feelings of pain, by sorrowing and mourning for them; but rather at once pass them over, and keep ourselves in the endless delight which is God.'

Trinity and
Unity

IN HIS CLASSIC WORK *WESTERN Mysticism* (1922), Dom Cuthbert Butler writes about Blessed Jan van Ruysbroek (1293–1381): 'In all probability there has been no greater contemplative; and certainly there has been no greater mystical writer.'

Butler is not alone in this assessment. Evelyn Underhill in *Mystics of the Church* (1925) writes as follows: 'Ruysbroek is one of the greatest—perhaps the greatest—of the mystics of the church. Ruysbroek's teaching cannot be summarized. No words other than his own can suggest its real quality, for it implies and proceeds from an experience of God which transcends the normal process of the mind. With each fresh reading it discloses fresh truths and secrets to those—and only those—who are ready to receive them. Increased familiarity with these writings brings a growing conviction that a real weight of meaning must be attached to every phrase, and that those which seem obscure to us are dark with excess of light. Ruysbroek is struggling to describe a genuine experience of Reality, so great when measured by our common human level, that the effort to understand him, to follow his ascent to 'that wayless being which all interior souls have chosen above all things' leaves us bewildered and awed'.

In his major work, *The Spiritual Espousals*, Ruysbroek treats in three books of The Active Life, The Interior Life and The Contemplative Life. He was no stranger to the first; for twenty-six years after ordination he served as a chaplain in Brussels before 'retiring' with a group of friends to nearby Groenendaal to devote himself to contemplation. 'The Interior Life' is by far the longest of Ruysbroek's three books, 'The Contemplative Life' by far the briefest. He presents each of the three books as a meditation on the text of Matthew's gospel: 'See; the Bridegroom is coming; go out to meet him' (Matthew 25:6).

The climax of Ruysbroek's reflections is his brief but dense treatment of contemplative life. In the preface he, like all the mystics, declares that contemplation is a gift, not attainable by any subtle reasonings or any exercises. He calls this gift of contemplation 'superessential' or 'divine'. 'To comprehend and understand God as he is in himself, above and beyond all likeness, is to be God with God, without intermediary or any element of otherness which could constitute an obstacle or impediment.' Aware of how easy it is to misinterpret such mystical language in an unorthodox sense, Ruysbroek appeals to his readers: 'I therefore beseech everyone who does not understand this or feel it in the blissful unity of his spirit not to take offence, but simply to let it be as it is'. Immediately he introduces his theme of the harmony between our participation in the active life of the Divine Persons and the unity of the Divine Being.

See. This word is spoken by the Father in the generation of the Son. The invitation calls us to both detachment and a clinging to God with intention and love. Thirdly, one must lose oneself in darkness; it is through this entry into darkness that God gifts us with revelation and with eternal life. 'In this darkness an incomprehensible light is born and shines forth; this is the Son of God in whom a person becomes able to see and contemplate eternal life.'

The Bridegroom is coming. The bridegroom comes as a 'revelation of eternal light ceaselessly renewed in the depth of the spirit'. All activity must cease, so that God alone is at work 'in the most sublime nobility of the spirit where there is only an eternal contemplating of and gazing at the light with the light and in the light'. The bridegroom both abides and ceaselessy comes anew.

Go out. The invitation to 'go out' is spoken by the Spirit of God within our own spirit. 'All the richness which is in God by nature is something which we lovingly possess in God—and God in us—through the infinite love which is the Holy Spirit.' As we go out into the darkness, our spirit is 'caught up into the embrace of the Holy Trinity'.

There is an eternal going forth and eternal activity within the persons of the Trinity. Through the eternal birth of the Son from the Father, 'all creatures have gone forth before their creation in time'. 'This eternal going forth and this eternal life which we eternally have and are in God apart from ourselves is a cause of our being created in time.'

This being so, God wills us to go out through contemplation to find the ground of our being in the bosom of the Father. To be raised to this contemplative life makes a person become 'one with the divine resplendence and become the divine resplendence itself'.

'Through an eternal act of gazing accomplished by means of the interior light contemplative persons are transformed and become one with that same light with which they see and which they see.' The contemplative life is the life of heaven, though, of course, our capacity for the divine light is greater when we are set free from this earthly exile.

To meet him. The meeting is in love. The divine activity in which the Father turns towards the Son and the Son towards the Father gives rise to the Holy Spirit, the love of both. How contradictory are the mystics! Ruysbroek declares that all creatures must remain silent before the embrace of the Spirit penetrating the Father and the Son, 'for the incomprehensible wonder that resides in this love eternally transcends the understanding of all creatures. But when a person *understands* this wonder and savours it without amazement, then has his spirit been raised above itself and made one with the Spirit of God.'

The glory of Ruysbroek is that he is able to spell out from his own experience the life of the Trinity received in Baptism. How thoroughly pauline he is in his incomparable understanding of the creation of all things in Christ (Colossians 1:16-20). How johannine in his appreciation of God's gifts of revelation and eternal life. While lyrically describing our participation in the active life of the Trinity, he keeps in perfect balance the negative way of mysticism that had come from pseudo-Dionysius. Through our contemplation we enter into the darkness of the Divine Unity, and there find blissful enjoyment.

Ruysbroek follows the teaching of Meister Eckhart (1260-1328) on the mystic's union with interpersonal life of the Trinity and with the darkness of the Divine Being. But he does this in a way that surpasses Eckhart in several respects. First, Ruysbroek is always keenly aware of the heretical tendencies to pantheism and quietism not uncommon among mystical writers of his time. He even produced a work, 'The Little Book of Clarification', explicity to defend himself against the possibility of any such charges. Yet Ruysbroek yields to no-one in his daring expressions of the oneness of the creature with God and the stilling of all activity. Thirdly, his writing never reads like theory divorced from his own profound, contemplative experience of the trinity and unity of God. In fact it has an unparallelled power to communicate that experience to his fortunate readers.

The simplicity of this 'greatest of mystics' is revealed in the concluding words of *The Spiritual Espousals*: 'That we might blissfully possess the essential Unity and clearly contemplate the Unity in the Trinity—may the divine love grant us this, for it turns no beggar away. Amen. Amen'.

God in
All Things

AFTER BEING WOUNDED IN BATTLE AT
the age of thirty, Ignatius of Loyola began a nine months' convales-
cence during which he underwent a radical conversion, brought about
through reading and praying over the Life of Christ and Lives of the
Saints. Not long into this period of conversion he experienced the
first of his visions: of Mary with the child Jesus in her arms. This had
the effect on him of making him despise his former loose living and
delivering him from his previous romantic imaginings. Ignatius, who
is often presented as a thinker, organizer, administrator and leader, is
far more a contemplative and mystic. And already we see what became a hallmark of Ignatius's mystical experiences: they had eminently
practical outcomes in his life.

Immediately after this conversion Ignatius spent ten months at
Manresa, near Barcelona, in intensive prayer and works of service in
hospitals. During this time his experience was of God schooling him
as a schoolteacher does with a pupil. Through contemplation God
and Ignatius were in immediate contact and continual relationship.
In his spoken autobiography Ignatius tells how at this time he had
five different outstanding mystical experiences or visions, both imaginative and intellectual: of the Trinity; of the creation of the world;

119

how Christ is present in the Blessed Sacrament; a vision with his 'interior eyes' of the humanity of Christ, an experience repeated up to forty times, along with similar visions of our Lady; and, finally, the greatest experience, the enlightenment that took place by the River Cardoner. The account of this last experience in the Autobiography is given above in the chapter 'Contemplative Prayer' (pp. 13–14). These experiences become powerfully influential in the life of Ignatius. His devotion to the Trinity and the humanity of Jesus dominate his prayer life from now on. The great vision by the river leads to what is often considered most characteristic of Ignatian spirituality, the phrase 'finding God in all things'.

At different times in his life, especially times of greatest difficulty, Ignatius refers to the presence of Christ with him constantly. 'He felt great consolation from our Lord, and it seemed to him that he saw Christ over him continually' (Jerusalem, 1523). 'He saw a vision of Christ being led away' (Spain, 1524). 'When he began to prepare for the priesthood at Venice and when he was preparing to say Mass and in all his journeys he had great supernatural visitations like those he used to have at Manresa' (1537). 'During the time he was at Vicenza he had many spiritual visions and ordinary consolations' (1537).

Finally, in that same year, as he was about to enter Rome, he stopped at the little wayside chapel at La Storta and repeated a prayer to Mary he had been saying constantly: 'Place me with your Son'. He then experienced not Mary, but the Father, placing him with his Son. This would lead to his founding in Rome an order to serve with Jesus under the symbol of the cross, and the giving of the name Society of Jesus to that order. Ignatius could not possibly allow a change of that name, because it had been given to him by God. Once again, we see the practical, down to earth effects of the mystical prayer life of Ignatius.

We have available some small sections of the Spiritual Diary of Ignatius for the years 1544-1545, some eleven years before his death. This was a time of intense personal involvement with the Most Holy Trinity, with Jesus and with Mary. He does not name the Holy Spirit separately, perhaps with an unerring theological instinct that all our praying is done in the Holy Spirit, who is so closely united to our own spirit that God's Spirit is not somebody 'out there' to whom we pray, but the one in whom all our praying is done. The spirituality of Ignatius at this time is dominated by the celebration of Mass and the contemplative experience during it of tears, so much so that he often had great difficulty in completing the Mass. He refers constantly to 'devotion', to 'familiarity with God' and to 'finding God'. Not only did he pause frequently throughout the day to reflect contemplatively on what God was doing in all the events of his life, but his constant preoccupation was thinking, talking, writing about God's presence and action.

Ignatius's spirituality was ruled by a powerful sense of mission and of labouring with Christ for the coming of the Kingdom in all of the practicalities of human living. As a result, the mysticism of Ignatius is often called a 'mysticism of service'. As one advances in union with God, contemplation does not require the spending of long hours in prayer; rather there is a growing facility to 'find God in all things'. This led one of the greatest of Ignatius's immediate companions, Jerome Nadal, to describe him as 'contemplative even in action'.

With his great sense of mission and apostolate, it is not surprising that Ignatius wished to share his contemplative experience with as many as possible. Immediately after his Manresa 'retreat' he set about doing this through spiritual conversation with anyone he met who was interested in prayer, but he was to reach many millions more people through his small book 'The Spiritual Exercises'. This is not a detailed analysis of what happens in contemplation, but a systematic leading of a person, as God had led him, through the stages of growth in spiritual life into deeper and deeper union. Each stage builds in dynamic fashion on what has preceded, so that reflection on the 'dynamic of the Spiritual Exercises' helps us to understand and appreciate their process.

In the writing of Ignatius it is often the small remark that has a basic, powerful and pervasive influence on all that follows. Here we look at some of these, giving them the numbers that belong to their particular numbered paragraph in the Spiritual Exercises.

'It is not to know much that fills and satisfies the soul, but to feel and to taste things interiorly' (2). Ignatius never rejects the intellect, but it is 'heart knowledge' that is the stuff of the Spiritual Exercises. Already the primacy of contemplation over all other forms of prayer begins to be hinted at. 'It will be very profitable to enter upon the Exercises with great magnanimity and generosity towards one's Creator and Lord, and to offer Him his entire will and liberty, that his Divine Majesty may dispose of him and all he possesses according to His most holy will' (5). All that follows will be enriched by the generosity of this starting disposition. In a list of 'helps to prayer' Ignatius directs that one should 'remain quietly meditating upon the point in which I have found what I desire, without any eagerness to move on till I have been satisfied' (76). This is a way of moving to that heart knowledge that satisfies the soul (2); it is the movement from meditation to contemplation.

Ignatius makes it clear throughout the Spiritual Exercises that he expects God to communicate Godself directly to each retreatant. Indeed, it was this kind of thinking that got him into repeated trouble with the Spanish Inquisition, and which led to a reaction within his own Society of Jesus to pull back from contemplation into the 'safer' ways of meditation. 'While one is engaged in the Spiritual Exercises, it is more suitable and much better that the Creator and Lord in person communicate Himself to the devout soul in quest of the divine will, that He inflame it with His love and praise, and dispose it for the way it could better serve God in the future. Therefore, the director of the Exercises, like a balance at equilibrium, without leaning to one side or the other, should permit the Creator and Lord to deal directly with the creature, and the creature directly with the Creator and Lord' (15).

In order to open oneself to the first and fundamental grace of the Spiritual Exercises, conversion of heart, Ignatius instructs us to reflect on our lives and to meditate upon sin and its forgiveness through the use of the three powers of the soul: memory, understanding and will. This is the adoption of the classical psychology of St Augustine, still in vogue at the time. Because this was the first way of praying recommended in the Exercises, in later thinking it became 'crystallized' as *the* Ignatian method of prayer.

Yet even at this stage of the Exercises, Ignatius recommends that as one advances one quickly leave behind meditation and return to the 'matter contemplated' (64). Moreover, each exercise is to lead the praying person into 'colloquy', dialogue or conversation, which will often take the form of an intimate exchange between friends, as in St

Teresa's explanation of contemplative prayer (*Catholic Catechism*, 2712), cited above in the chapter 'Contemplative Prayer'. For Ignatius, 'The colloquy is made by speaking exactly as one friend speaks to another' (54). The grace of conversion is only receivable through union with God in Christ The experience of this gift can be attained only in contemplation.

When the person making the Exercises has come through the initial phase of conversion, they are invited to focus on the person of Christ in the 'Kingdom' meditation and begin to make a totally generous offering of self in going Christ's way to bring about the coming of the Kingdom. This is the way of self-emptying and self-sacrifice, achievable only through a profound union of love, the stuff of contemplation. From this point on, the prayer of the Exercises becomes contemplation of the mysteries of the life of Christ, in order to know, love and to follow him (104). This prayer remains the same throughout the mysteries of the life of Christ up to his Passion (76). The 'heart knowledge' sought is that of Paul in Philippians 3:10: 'All I want is to know Christ and the power of his resurrection and to share his sufferings by reproducing the pattern of his death'.

Only rarely, when dealing with reflection on the practicalities of one's life and seeking an understanding of the application of the Gospel to these, as in the 'Two Standards', does Ignatius recommend a return to discursive meditation. Here again, as in the conversion phase, he expects a movement into contemplation. After the first discursive meditation of Two Standards, there are to be three 'repetitions'. These are contemplations. 'I will make use of the same three colloquies employed in the preceding *contemplation* on Two Standards' (156).

For Ignatius, 'repetition' is a technical term meaning a dwelling on consolation or desolation previously experienced: in order to overcome the desolation; in order to deepen the consolation. Consolation, a movement of the whole person, feeling, affectivity and will towards God is a contemplative experience:

'I call it consolation when an interior movement is aroused in the soul, by which it is inflamed with love of its Creator and Lord, and as a consequence, can love no creature on the face of the earth for its own sake, but only in the Creator of them all. It is likewise consolation when one sheds tears that move to the love of God, whether it be because of sorrow for sins, or because of the sufferings of Christ our Lord, or for any other reason that is immediately directed to the praise and service of God. Finally, I call consolation every increase of faith, hope and love, and all interior joy that invites and attracts to what is heavenly and to the salvation of one's soul by filling it with peace and quiet in its Creator and Lord' (316).

Ignatius gives two different sets of 'rules' or guidelines for the discernment of spirits. Immediately after the first, conversion, phase of the Exercises, Ignatius introduces the notion of 'consolation without any previous cause'. 'It belongs solely to the Creator and Lord to come into a soul, to leave it, to act upon it, to draw it wholly to the love of His Divine Majesty. I said without previous cause, that is, without any preceding perception or knowledge of any subject by which a soul might be led to such a consolation through its own acts of intellect and will' (330). It is clear that Ignatius allows for, even expects, this direct self-communication of God to the praying person. It describes a sheerly gratuitous gift of union, such as understood by the classic term 'infused contemplation'.

The fruit of the meditation on the Two Standards and the ensuing repetitions is to be received under the standard of Christ (the Cross) in the highest spiritual poverty. In dealing with the passive dark night of the spirit in *Dark Night* (2.4.1), John of the Cross sees the contemplative purgation involved as equivalent to nakedness or poverty of spirit. The prayer of Ignatius is no less radical than that of John. Nor should we expect it to be. Both are concerned with facing up to the most radical demands of the Gospel. The function of contemplation in the second, or discipleship, phase of the Spiritual Exercises is to lead a person to a radical freedom in Christ, which will enable them to make decisions based solely on the promptings of God's Spirit.

The closeness of the union with Christ envisaged is most strongly underlined in Ignatius's presentation of Three Degrees of Humility. A person habitually in the second degree is living in such a way that no creature holds them captive and they are free to choose only what God wants. Surely there cannot be a third degree beyond this! Rationally there cannot. In the language of contemplative love there is. A person living habitually in the third degree of humility is not just free, but has a bias towards choosing in the way in which Christ chose. There is a bias, coming from love, towards poverty, humiliations and humility in preference to wealth, honours and pride.

In the dynamic of the Spiritual Exercises one who has received these kinds of gifts from God is now ready to enter the contemplation of the Lord's sufferings death and resurrection in the highest degrees of contemplative union. On going through the contemplation of the death and resurrection of Christ in this way, one is now able to become aware of the presence of God in every aspect and detail of one's life.

Ignatius sums this up, and climaxes the whole process of his Exercises, with his great and final 'Contemplation to Attain the Love of God'. The person is now able to live in a total exchange of gratitude and self-giving with God the giver of all gifts. They see God as present in every aspect of their living, as ceaselessly working to communicate with them, and they see everything as an expression of God's self-gift. The response that comes from the human heart is to make a total return of all that one is and has to God. The essence of this reponse is summed up in the prayer of Ignatius: 'Take, Lord, and accept all my liberty, my memory, my understanding, and my entire will, all that I have and possess. You have given all to me. To You, O Lord, I return it all. All is Yours, dispose of it wholly according to Your will. Give me Your love and Your grace, for this is sufficient for me' (234).

Notice that the wording used here is the same as in paragraph 5 of the Spiritual Exercises, quoted above. We have returned to our beginnings. The reality hasn't changed; it is just that we now relate to it in a totally new depth of contemplation.

The 'Contemplation to Attain the Love of God' leads a person more and more to be able, in Ignatius's classic phrase, to 'find God in all things'. His thought on the right attitude of the human person to God and creation is most beautifully expressed in his writing in the Constitutions of the Society of Jesus: 'In all things let them seek God, casting off the love of all creatures to the extent that this is possible, so that they may give their whole affection to the Creator of them, loving Him in all creatures and them all in Him, according to His most holy and divine will' (Constitutions 288).

In a Dark Night

FOR ST JOHN OF THE CROSS, contemplation is that phase of our prayer-journey which begins after we have passed through the often delightful stages of our relationship with God to a time in which we are are simply present in loving attention to the God who is beyond all our experience, beyond our words, thoughts, feelings, desires. The cornerstone of John's doctrine on prayer is this transition from meditation (use of thoughts and images) to contemplation (simply remaining in loving attention to God's presence).

There are three signs that a person is making this transition:
1. I cannot meditate. Attempts at meditation lead only to dryness.
2. I have no wish to fix my imagination on any particular object.
3. (And this is the indispensable test) I like to remain in a general, loving awareness of God without any particular acts.

All three signs must be present simultaneously. The first and second are never sufficient to indicate this transition.

We enter contemplation after a time of initial purgation. All relationship with God that we might be able to feel or perceive must be let go. Not only that: all relationship with God in the depth of our spirit must be let go. We must be detached from spiritual possessions, spiritual experience. We must even reject divine communications. Now that faith is perfected, we have no need for divine inner words, visions, raptures or spiritual feelings. In refusing to accept these we do not thereby destroy the fruit that God wants for us.

The way for John is the way of detachment and of faith. These two words are the key to appreciating his writings. If we lose sight of his total commitment to 'detachment', the words of the great poet and passionate lover of nature can seem positively manichean. John never tires of stressing that the dark and secure way of Faith is the *only* proximate way to union with God. Nothing else can put us immediately in touch with God. Paradoxically it is through this darkness that we experience the one who 'dwells in inaccessible light'.

'There is nothing in contemplation or the divine inflow which of itself can give pain; contemplation rather bestows sweetness and delight. The cause for not experiencing these agreeable effects is the soul's weakness and imperfection at the time, its inadequate preparation, and the qualities it possesses which are contrary to this light. Because of this the soul has to suffer when the divine light shines upon it' (*Dark Night*, 2.9.11). So, the way of contemplation necessarily becomes the way of *darkness*.

Although God is manifested to the soul 'by means of faith, in divine light exceeding all understanding' (*Ascent of Mt Carmel*. 2.9.1), it is precisely because it exceeds all understanding that the experience is one of darkness. John goes on in this chapter to show how God is presented in scripture as appearing in darkness, because God can be encountered in this life only in the obscurity of faith.

Detachment demands that we take *nothing* with us on the ascent of Mount Carmel: nothing that we can sense, nothing in the higher powers of our spirit; moreover, we must expect to find *nothing* when we reach the summit. As we go forward, we are purified—become more detached—through the active and passive nights of sense, and the active and passive nights of spirit. John makes it perfectly clear that these are not to be thought of as four distinct, consecutive stages. We do make progress in the life of the Spirit, but never in linear fashion. We make our efforts to be detached both in sense and in spirit; God is working, freeing us in sense and spirit. The way of thinking in which we have been educated leads us to tend to 'objectify' such schematic presentations as that of the four dark nights.

Similarly, it would be a sad impoverishment to obscure the treasures of the Spiritual Canticle by fixating on John's schematic use of the classic purgative, illuminative and unitive ways. I may be tempted to ask myself if I have passed from one to the other. Such a question is futile. To pray with John of the Cross is certainly not to force myself to fit into an intellectual schematization that John employs in his very systematic style of writing. Moreover, John himself insists that 'God leads each one along different paths, so that hardly one spirit will be found like another in even half its method of procedure' (*Living Flame*, 3. 59).

Through contemplation there is an inflow into the soul of God, who is light and love. Because of our weakness and our sinfulness, this divine inflow is experienced as darkness. 'God is intolerable darkness to the soul when spiritually near, for the supernatural light darkens with its excess the natural light' (*Spiritual Canticle*, 13:1). John leads us on the *secure* path of darkness. His personal experience, especially of imprisonment and psychological torture, certainly pointed him in this direction. He is a living witness to his title 'of the Cross'. But his spirituality cannot, of course, be more radical than the uncompromising demands of the gospel. When treating of the deepest darkness, he remarks that 'contemplative purgation is nothing other than poverty of spirit' (*Dark Night*, 2.4.1). To be a disciple is to take up one's cross, even to lose one's life.

The negative is never sought after for its own sake. It is, for John, the way to the transforming union and the delight of the spiritual marriage. Nor is the resurrection ever separate from the cross throughout the process. All through his writing, John tells of the delight that is present even in the darkest experiences. Night, for John, passes through varying degrees of darkness; and, of course, night is always followed by dawn. Although the experience of the dark night is 'bitter and terrible to the sense' and even more 'horrible and frightful to the spirit', in his commentary on the first stanza of his poem of the Dark Night John declares that in entering upon this night 'the soul begins the sweet and delightful life of love with God' (*Dark Night*, Explanation 1).

There will be intervals of 'the sweetness of peace and loving friendship with God', in the middle of times of great affliction (*Dark Night*, 2.7.4). 'Even though this *happy* night darkens the spirit, it does so only to impart light concerning all things; and even though it humbles a person and reveals his miseries, it does so only to exalt him; and even though it impoverishes and empties him of all possessions and natural affections, it does so only that he may reach out divinely to all things, with a general freedom of spirit in them all' (*Dark Night*. 2.9.1).

Though the conscious experience be one of darkness and pain, the delight is present with it, sometimes breaking through into our consciousness. Such delight is not sought, but is received from God in perfect detachment. The heart of the matter is that there is no other way to wisdom than the cross. If you want wisdom, you will first long for the cross.

The whole process of mystical theology, or contemplation, is an entry into a secret wisdom that comes from God and fills the person with delight. 'The sweet and living knowledge she says He taught her is mystical theology, that secret knowledge of God which spiritual persons call contemplation. This knowledge is very delightful because it is knowledge through love. Love is the master of this knowledge and that which makes it wholly agreeable. Since God communicates this knowledge and understanding in the love with which He communicates Himself to the soul, it is very delightful to the intellect, since it is a knowledge belonging to the intellect, and it is delightful to the will since it is communicated in love, which pertains to the will' (*Spiritual Canticle*, 27. 5).

In his poem on the Canticle and its commentary John describes the effects that come from the journey through night: spiritual marriage and the transforming union of love. 'This spiritual marriage is incomparably greater than the spiritual espousal, for it is a total transformation in the Beloved in which each surrenders the entire possession of self to the other with a certain consummation of the union of love. The soul thereby becomes divine, becomes God through participation, in so far as is possible in this life' (*Spiritual Canticle*, 22:3).

Surely John has reached the pinnacle of Christian life. But, no, there is a further poem and commentary, because we can go on growing in the quality and depth of our union through becoming a living flame of divine love.

John commences his commentary on the Living Flame of Love by declaring that the flame is the Holy Spirit. Whereas earlier, in the dark night, the effect of the fire was to blacken the wood and make it give off smoke and even a foul smell, now the effect of this divine fire on the soul is to make it alive and incandescent.

'Although in the stanzas we have already commented on [the Spiritual Canticle], we speak of the highest degree of perfection we can reach in this life [transformation in God], these stanzas treat of a love within this very state of transformation that has a deeper quality and is more perfect. Even though it is true that what these and the other stanzas describe is all one state of transformation, and that as such one cannot pass beyond it, yet, with time and practice, love can receive added quality, and become more intensified. Although the fire has penetrated the wood, transformed it, and united it with itself, yet as this fire grows hotter and continues to burn, the wood becomes much more incandescent and inflamed, even to the point of flaring up and shooting out flames from itself' (*Living Flame*, Prologue 3).

Already, on earth, the person has passed through purgatory in the dark night. 'In so far as infused contemplation is loving wisdom of God, it produces two principal effects in the soul: it prepares the soul for the union with God through love both by purging and illumining it. Hence the same loving wisdom that purges and illumines the blessed spirits, purges and illumines the soul here on earth' (*Dark Night*, 2.5.1).

As this union continues to grow now in the living flame, the person moves closer and closer to the glory of the Beatific Vision. 'Such is the glory this flame of love imparts that it each time it absorbs and attacks, it seems that it is about to give eternal life and tear the veil of mortal life, that very little is lacking, and that because of this lack the soul does not receive eternal glory completely' (*Living Flame*, 1:1). By the end of the Living Flame John is very fittingly reduced to *silence*. All words are inadequate.

Wells and
Cloudbursts
and Mansions

IN HER AUTOBIOGRAPHY (CHAPTER 11) St Teresa begins to describe her experience of stages of growth in prayer, drawing on the beautiful imagery of a garden of flowers in need of watering. She describes four different kinds of watering: first, taking water from a well; second, having the use of a water wheel and its buckets to draw the water; third, being gifted with a stream of water; fourth, receiving the heavy rain of cloudbursts.

Teresa is picturing for us a growth which clears the way more and more for the praying person to receive the divine initiative of our ever-loving God.

First watering. This is the prayer of beginners. It will involve much review of one's past life and the effort to meditate on the life of Christ It may often be very dry, so that there is great need for fortitude and humility.

Second watering. Here we have the Prayer of Recollection, leading to the Prayer of Quiet, in which the will is quiet, wanting only what God wants, though the memory and understanding are not under control. There is still a mixture of the natural and supernatural, a word which Teresa uses to mean sheer, infused gift through no effort of ours. She declares that many reach this stage of the second watering, but few go beyond it.

Third watering. Here Teresa describes several different kinds of prayer of union with God. There is 'a union of the whole soul with God', though not yet complete union. As in the Prayer of Quiet, the will is in union 'captive and rejoicing', but the memory and understanding are left free.

Fourth watering. This is the Prayer of Union, properly so called. God unites the whole soul to Godself, with its faculties in union: senses, memory and understanding are now at one with the will. In this state one cannot read a single letter or frame a single word. The understanding cannot comprehend, much less communicate what is happening. There is a new kind of rejoicing, not so much felt, but wholly caused by God's intervention. Union of the faculties occurs only for short intervals, no more than half an hour at most. The will remains quiet, as in the Prayer of Quiet, but the other faculties move in and out of union. Within the Prayer of Union there is sometimes given the gift of rapture, or flight of spirit, or elevation of spirit.

Later, in her most systematic work, the Interior Castle, Teresa develops her teaching of stages of prayer through the use of the seven different kinds of mansions of the castle.

First. Prayer and meditation are the way into the castle. The person in these mansions prays occasionally.

Second. This is the way of self-knowledge and humility. There is a readiness to respond to God's invitations to leave aside pleasure and strive to conform to God's will.

Third. The state of the Rich Young Man, observing the commandments, but fearful of the next step. The call to complete self-renunciation versus the danger of back-sliding. There is need for a good spiritual director.

Fourth. This is prayer touching on the 'supernatural', that is, infused. First comes the Prayer of Recollection, seeking God within ourselves, not by thinking or imagination, but by a *gift* of absorption. This leads to the Prayer of Quiet, in which the will is united to God, the other faculties remaining free to wander. We do not try to stop thinking, though thought may cease for a while. We gently stop discursive prayer. Another term for Prayer of Quiet is consolation from God, with the effect of dilating the heart, increasing virtue. The Prayer of Quiet doesn't happen just once or twice, but we continue to receive it. Most persons of prayer enter these fourth mansions. Here nature and supernature are both at work, so there remains scope for the attacks of the evil spirit.

Fifth. The prayer of these mansions is the Prayer of Union. It is a union of the whole soul with God. It lasts for moments; perhaps never more than half an hour. The soul is asleep or dead to the world. It must face great trials, for there is nowhere to settle. When this union has occurred, it is impossible to doubt it, even though there is no experience to remember. It demands as its sign perfect love of neighbour.

Sixth. These are the places of spiritual betrothal. This is the time of the wound of love, and of great trials. The sense of sin is heightened. But the wounding is more satisfying than stressless Prayer of Quiet. The person hears the Spouse calling from the seventh mansions. There is the pain of intense desire, accompanied by tranquillity and joy. In these mansions Teresa reflects upon: locutions and the principles for their discernment; rapture or ecstasy, which is a confirmation of the betrothal; imaginary visions, which are not to be sought; and intellectual visions, such as her suddenly seeing all things in God; and flight of spirit. There can be such joy that one is compelled to share it. The need remains to keep in touch with the humanity of Christ. Each favour causes fresh pain. There can be a near-death experience, involving dislocation of limbs. The person experiences the anguish of being in love, but separated from the Beloved. Life is torture, so there is a longing for death. Great courage is required to enter these mansions!

Seventh. The place of the Spiritual Marriage. It often commences with an intellectual vision of the Trinity. The promised communion of the seventeenth chapter of John's gospel is fulfilled. The person is not lost in absorption, but alert for *service*. It is truly a marriage. The two are now one. There is habitual, constant companionship. There is abiding love in the soul, though not in the faculties; so that exterior trials and attacks of the enemy remain; one may even sin. Rarely are there disturbances and aridity, as in the previous mansions. Raptures are very rare. In place of weakness comes strength. Previously the person wished to die; now the desire is to live for many years in service. The fruit is humility and loving service of the neighbour, with one's eyes fixed on the crucified Christ

It should be obvious from these accounts that Teresa is writing in a very vivid way about her own personal experience, rather than laying down guidelines for all to follow. What a contrast between the effusive, personal, often humourous, Teresa and the analytic, systematic John of the Cross. We should always allow their strikingly feminine and masculine approaches to complement each other. We must avoid the temptation to try to work out some kind of objective synthesis, attempting, for instance, to identify Teresa's Prayer of Quiet with John's prayer of loving attention, or the pain of the sixth mansions with the dark night of the spirit. Rather, I simply allow each of these great mystics to speak to my own experience in whatever way the writing of either becomes relevant to me personally.

While the schematic development of the mansions marks a real, continuing growth in prayer, which normally takes place over many years, God may still gift people with the higher, later forms of prayer even from the start. This is what Teresa reports in her own case. She received the gift of the sixth mansions very early in her religious life. Her response to this gift was for many years inadequate, but at the time of her 'conversion' at the age of thirty-nine, became whole-hearted.

Teresa's writing, like John's, is dominated by cross-resurrection. She always respects the divine initiative of the God who can intervene with cloudbursts upon our feeble attemps to draw water from the well. Not for Teresa the pain of darkness, but she is open to the equally crucifying pain of unrequited love. Throughout the times of dryness, trials and attacks of the evil spirit, the delight involved in the whole process of response to God's loving gifts is always present. This is revealed not only in Teresa's words, but in her whole lightsome, happy style of writing. She reveals throughout her worthiness of the title 'Teresa of Jesus', as one who is truly at home with Jesus.

Postscript

IT HAS BEEN THIS BOOK'S AIM TO OPEN up and to deepen the understanding that contemplation is not an esoteric prayer form reserved for some special people 'out there'. It is, in fact, a natural gift given to every person on this planet. It is a gift that needs to be responded to and developed by consciously giving time to prayer. Once again, this does not involve a special style or technique. It requires entry into one's heart to meet the God who is already at home there. All authentic prayer has this heart dimension, and is therefore, at least inchoately, contemplative.

For a Christian, the development of a life of contemplative prayer is a response to and activization of one's Baptism. This does not remain a 'dead letter', gathering dust in some church ledger, but comes alive each time I enter the dwelling place of Father, Son and Holy Spirit: my own heart.

When we turn to Scripture, we experience the need to read it contemplatively. When we look into the New Testament, we find that the example of the prayer of Jesus and of St Paul and the constant teaching on prayer all point us in the direction of contemplation. We see that the Lord's Prayer and the prayer of Jesus before his death and resurrection are one and the same. The Christian, in union with Jesus, prays in the Spirit to the Father to establish God's reign in our world.

The introduction to some of the great historical ways of Chistian contemplation is in no sense an abrupt break with the scriptural part of this book. From the *lectio divina* of the sixth century to St Teresa of Avila in the seventeenth, all Christian contemplation has a close unity with its scriptural roots. No contemplative or mystic could ever go beyond what is available to the whole church in the Word of God. Scripture has established for all time the parameters of all Christian prayer.

The most profound ways of contemplation are seen to be essentially simple, and, according to God's gift, possible to all. The prayer of a John of the Cross, a Julian of Norwich or Ignatius of Loyola is often shared by very ordinary people, without their being aware of the fact.

May our reading encourage each of us on our journey to develop our own personal gift of prayer, in the sure belief that it is in touch with the Word of God and our great Christian tradition.